Working MUM SURVIVAL GUIDE

Working MUM SURVIVAL GUIDE

P DAVIS

Vitasta

Published by
Renu Kaul Verma
Vitasta Publishing Pvt Ltd
2/15, Ansari Road, Daryaganj
New Delhi - 110 002
info@vitastapublishing.com

ISBN: 978-81-963329-7-6

First Edition 2024
MRP ₹399

Edited by Soumitro Das
Typeset & Cover Design by Somesh Kumar Mishra
Printed by Vikas Computer and Printers, New Delhi

Contents

Foreword

This book has been written to raise awareness about the difficulties of maintaining work-life balance in a modern household. As a woman, I feel it is important to feel empowered to manage your household in a way that addresses the emotional, physical as well as social needs of your family unit whilst working to earn a living.

I dedicate this book to our close friends and family who have stuck with us through thick and thin (psst... you know who you all are!).

I also want to pay tribute to my grandfather, George Puran Singh and grandmother, Gracie Singh, who are sadly no longer with us, whose love and humility will never be forgotten. Their memories are the glue that keep us together and their legacy will remain with us forever.

Nana and Nani, *phir milenge*.

Chapter 1

Juggling work and family

I am no stranger to working life. I come from a family of hard-working professionals. My father was a doctor, my mother ran a kindergarten school and took tuition classes. My grandfather took spoken English classes, ran a primary school and saw it grow from strength to strength into a full-sized academy. People tell me that he used to stand with a placard attached to his shirt advertising *The A-B-C School*, which was eventually renamed, the Eden's. So, my point is, I did not become a working mum out of the blue.

You see, having gotten married in my early twenties, my husband and I had to learn to support ourselves. Living in a Western country, both partners in a marriage have to work to support a family. Rent is hard to pay, bills even harder! Forget about extra perks like fancy restaurants and cinemas.

Adjusting to life after marriage, sustaining a full time job and BOOM!, we find out we're pregnant (yes, I said, 'we' not 'I' since my husband is an equal contributor as a hands-on parent!)

So, fast forward a decade and a half and two gorgeous children later, here I am, writing about how to deal with the stresses of juggling work and family.

In my years of travelling backwards and forwards to India, I can't help but notice the difference in the mentality of working families now and when I used to live in India many, many, years ago.

I am referring to a time when there were no electronic tablets, mobile phones, 24-hour cable TV etc. Instead, we had long power cuts, noisy neighbours, mosquitoes and no air conditioning. A time when you had to get up at 4.30 am, shower and catch your school bus at 6.30 am, be back home at 2 pm, shower again, lunch, an afternoon siesta (which I hated!), and around 4 pm the tutor was already ringing the bell. After that you could enjoy a nice game of cricket or badminton in the gully before dinner. Evenings were spent with family, playing *antakshari* and word games on the terrace underneath a starlit sky.

Reality hits home

All that is over and done with. With gadgets taking over our lives, I haven't been a role model. Just like everyone else, I respond to my child's questions without looking up from my phone. Then guilt strikes and I try to check myself, 'I'm sorry, darling, say that again?'

We enjoy the modern conveniences of life. It's great to wake up to the smell of freshly brewed coffee, have Bluetooth connectivity in the car, Netflix to entertain us, Amazon for instant dopamine hits and those fantastically depressing news channels. Everything is 'smart' but we're still living in a world full of dumb people!

In fact, we all know those moments when we're in a rush – and we mix up the names of all our other siblings or children? Well, I often end up calling out Alexa's name too. Not Alexa as in daughter or sibling, but as in Alexa the dot speaker!

Where do we fit in?

In the many experiences I have come across both in person and on paper, parents everywhere try to instil the same ethics in our children: Study hard, work hard. Yes, we may have all seen Bollywood movies suggesting life changes like *3 Idiots* and *Taare Zameen Par* but honestly, how often do we stop and consider where do we fit, where do our children fit in our lifestyle? Sure, every loving parent wants the best for their children, but what does that mean? Wanting the best for your child can mean different things to different people. It can be influenced by a number of things, such as society, our own upbringing and families and the individual needs of the child. If you had to choose, how would you *prioritise* what you wish to provide for your child, among the following?

- Good education
- Morals and values

- Designer clothing and/or the latest gadgets
- Great holidays
- Emotional, physical and mental stimulation

Many of my clients, find themselves at a crossroads when they become parents. They often find themselves becoming anxious at the thought of becoming a parent. They want to do the best for their child but don't know where to start. Consider these thoughts:

- ✓ What kind of parent do I wish to be?
- ✓ Should I be a strict, no-nonsense parent?
- ✓ Or should I be a relaxed and easy- going parent? What role does emotional connection play within a family?
- ✓ Is it possible to be a relaxed but not 'over lax' parent?

Chapter 2

Teaching them life skills and values

Whatever our parenting ideas or hopes and dreams for our children there are some things I always recommend to my clients.

A. Every child is unique with their own unique set of emotional, physical and mental needs. I know from experience. You may think that you only need advice if you're a first-time Mum and after that, parenting becomes easier for the second child. Could I have been more wrong? My first born is very different from my second born. Difference in age aside, both children have unique personalities and emotional requirements; parenting techniques that work with one do not necessarily work with the other.

   I have had to make my peace with the fact that

as a parent you are always learning and growing. Just when you think you've figured it out, you come across something you've never dealt with before and then boom! You start all over again.

B. Encourage, not force, the habit of studying. Yes, of course, like all loving parents, I too, want my children to excel in their studies and become academic achievers. When your child comes home with A+ grades on their subjects you want to show it off to your friends and family, don't you? I know I certainly do! Speaking for my husband and I, in addition to excellent basic education, we would like our child to also benefit from mental and physical stimulation. As they grow older and their educational choices for college or university become more streamlined, I passionately believe in encouraging my kids to achieve a skilled qualification in addition to their chosen and compulsory subjects. For example, we expect our son to complete his education - that goes without saying. However my husband and I have also encouraged him to qualify in a recognised skill with which he could start to earn a living straight after finishing his studies if he wanted to. After that, he is free to pursue his goals in a field of his choice after having secured a steady fallback in place.

C. Encourage them to take an active interest in sports or athletics. I am not just talking about getting them to like or follow a certain game on television as an enthusiastic spectator. Get them physically involved or better still, join them! Check out your neighbourhood recommendations for sporting options, whether it is swimming, tennis, cricket, badminton, football, jogging or even if it is just skipping rope. The key here is not only to give them the options available but also to *get them to choose*, even if it is just one activity. As they grow older and more independent, they will benefit from having a physical activity they love. This active involvement will teach them sportsmanship, teamwork, perseverance, confidence, as well as how to cope with anxiety and stress.

D. When children develop hobbies, it helps their mental wellbeing and confidence and develops excellent motor skills. Our son learnt to play the guitar and loves knitting and making superheroes from loom bands and now his interest has moved on to computers, putting old PCs together as also taking them apart. Creativity, productivity, developing fine motor skills all in one go! My daughter has also developed a love for several string instruments, painting, and baking.

The bottom line remains the same. Each child is unique. Surely, you will need to tailor your parenting style for each one to bring out the best in them and to help them grow up to be well rounded adults.

Whether you are a working Mum in India or any other country, I find that the following holds true across the board.

Mums (and Dads) fulfil so many roles in their daily lives. Whether it is being a friend, a teacher, a comforter, a disciplinarian, a first aider or even a chauffeur; the list is simply endless. One thing that has stayed with me throughout my working life is that regardless of where you live on the planet or your background, if you become a parent, chances are that you will be fulfilling at least some of the above roles if not all simultaneously.

The question arises: how can you fulfil your role as a working parent without compromising both spaces? Do you need to follow the age-old patterns that our parents used to follow? Do we need to raise our children in the same way we were raised? The world is now a much smaller place. Would it be reasonable to perhaps take a fresh look at the times we're living in now with a focus on the challenges our children are facing now as opposed to challenges *we* faced when *we* were young?

To address this, let's look at the similarities between Indian and western countries.

Chapter 3

Differences in families

Families in western countries

Children can usually enjoy good quality state education, healthcare as well as a range of systems including personalised support for various learning and physical or emotional difficulties; young people have numerous choices in terms of work experience, be it part time, full time or during school holidays etc. Both parents must work to support the family; most working families are tied down to huge mortgage or rent commitments and monthly bills must be cared for as well. Not to mention, yearly childcare costs can add up to a small fortune.

If you are fortunate, retired grandparents will be on hand to greatly help with childcare. There can also usually be flexibility with employers who will allow you to work from home or work during school hours, which can be a godsend if you cannot afford to pay for childcare and do not have the luxury of having family help. Once you're home from work and school pickup, there's dinner to be prepared, laundry to be done, clothes to be ironed, homework to be assisted with, uniforms and school lunches made ready for the next day, washing up to be done (did I say that again? Sorry, it must be the exhaustion talking!)

Did I mention grocery shopping and putting away all that shopping, vacuuming floors, washing the dishes (yes more washing!), feeding, and bathing the children, clearing up, 10 minutes of rest, go to bed and yes, the same routine the next day and the day after. Weekends are usually spent in volunteer work if you're into that kind of thing, shopping, extracurricular activities, mowing the lawn, cleaning the cars, more washing. By the end of Sunday evening, you cannot believe how quickly the weekend has flown by. In this type of hectic routine, it is no wonder that families look forward to their annual holiday during the summer and if they are fortunate, a couple of weekends away in between. Not surprising that they call it a holiday even if it wasn't HOLY!

Families in the Indian subcontinent

While many family units living in cosmopolitan cities must work full time to support themselves, others are fortunate to have a good support system in the form of a joint family.

By this I mean, the grandparents assisting with care

of the children, usually from the moment they are born until they finish school. Having observed and heard of experiences of so many families, this has proved to be a boon for working parents, particularly as they can trust their parents/in laws to care for their children properly while Mummy and Daddy are at work.

Most families can afford some domestic help full time or more usually part time in India. This is something my 17-year-old son could not understand at first as he could not imagine someone being called a 'servant' in a household. In his opinion, the idea of domestic 'servants' should have been abolished during the British Raj!

Nevertheless, for me as a mother, having a domestic worker can be a boon when raising a family. You can unload yourself of some extra stress and mundane jobs around the house as well as provide employment opportunities to the less advantaged in society.

How my experience compares

My husband and I worked full time and managed to buy our first house. When we had our first child, our son, I didn't have a domestic worker. In fact, we were quite hard up and we decorated our apartment all by ourselves. I'm not just talking about painting the walls or putting up new wallpaper. I am talking about tiling the bathroom (while 8 months pregnant by the way, but hey, one more thing I can tick off my bucket list), putting down new flooring, etc (courtesy my jack-of-all trades husband).

Yes, we have had a great network of friends who

helped us out in other specialized aspects such as, plumbing, electrical work, etc. My in-laws arrived and on one of those days that I was painting the walls, the baby decided to arrive 3 weeks earlier than expected! I did not have anyone to help with the baby or the housework or the cooking, the washing up, the laundry, the works. But who cared? My baby was here and I was determined I would be a good mother.

A boy and a girl later and having been blessed with a husband of 20 years standing, I can honestly say, together we have stuck through thick and thin. Having experienced plenty of hardships and difficulties over the years, we now run a successful and busy childcare centre and while we have always tried our best to keep our small family happy, it is still a work in progress. I can't lie, it's quite tiring, but what you sow with your children in their younger years you will reap later. I do NOT mean financial dividends, I mean that your children will likely grow up to be responsible and generous, hardworking, and kind humans and members of society.

External influences

As you may have gathered by now, my husband and I have our own little family unit where we have had to learn the ropes through trial and error. We have a great friend circle, mainly families with similar interests and children of a similar age and we don't need to spend too much energy and money on external childcare or assistance.

It may sound weird, but I found that before we had

children, our social circle was mainly formed by other single friends or married couples of a similar age group. Once we had children, it became difficult to maintain the same social circle. You end up meeting other couples or families with children regardless of the age difference. You find you have more in common with this new circle of people who don't seem to mind you talking about your child's potty-training sessions or a snotty nose incident, etc.

It becomes easier to relate with people who are living the same adventures day-in-and-day-out as you are and your children and their children keep themselves busy and entertained with each other during outings and visits. This is a major bonus!

Having said that, we do regularly keep in touch with our older friends who have decided for one reason or another not to have children yet. There are also those couples who would love to have their own children, but biology has failed them. When they spend time with our kids, they can temporarily fill that void. We have friends who are old enough to be our kids' adopted grandparents and they large-heartedly love and spoil them. Even if our kids miss those really important family relationships of grandparents living nearby or meeting their cousins or aunts and uncles daily, they don't lose out on the love.

Chapter 4

Keep them grounded

Like all parents, I love my children. They mean the world to me. I would do anything for them. Whatever be the nature of my job, or the hours I spend at work, deciding on childcare options, moving houses, changing schools, all our decisions are made around our children. Why?

Because they are not insignificant, tiny, and helpless humans living with us; they are our responsibilities. They are our pride and joy – true blessings from the Creator of Life. They deserve the best. You want to be the best parent you can be.

However, a wise man once gave me a pearl of wisdom, *never compare yourself to another parent*, be it your own parents, your in-laws, or your friends. It puts too much pressure on you, resulting in feelings of inadequacy and unnecessary guilt when you could actually be enjoying and cherishing the time you have with your children. Rather, when you compare yourself to your own past self, you can avoid repeating the mistakes you may have made. You will surely improve as you move forward in life.

Although I want my children to have the best experiences in life, I never want to shield them from a measure of hardship and disappointment in life. Why do I say that? Call it tough love, but I personally believe that giving them movie – inspired ideologies like, 'follow your dreams' or, 'you can get anything you want in life' can send them out into the world with unrealistic expectations. When an adolescent goes out into the world, not achieving what they've been dreaming of can be very disappointing and humiliating. I would instead prefer to foster realistic behaviour in my children by following the principle, 'Set a goal, work hard and don't give up trying'. If you teach them to appreciate the value of hard work, sincerity and perseverance, when the right opportunity comes along, they can grab hold of it with their eyes open instead of expecting everything to happen effortlessly.

Chapter 5

Love or obligation – raising children in a changing culture

As in most traditional societies worldwide, so in India people prefer boys over girls because of the dowry system or because people expect boys to grow up to provide financial support for the whole family. If a woman isn't able to conceive a boy she is often ridiculed or subject to the worst forms of cruel and inhumane treatment.

In many places around the world, if you had a daughter, often she was just tolerated, not loved, and appreciated as much as a son, which is such a shame as both genders deserve the same love and care. I am the second child of three siblings, my sister being the oldest and my brother the youngest. Growing up, my sister and I were never treated as being inferior to my brother or male cousins. I am grateful to my family that we were exposed to the same opportunities in life as my male relatives.

I remember noticing my female classmates often feeling dejected for being treated lesser than their male siblings.

With a wider educational reach, things are starting to move forward in the right direction in terms of gender preference. These days, most families are quite happy to have a child or a grandchild of either gender. Extended families and in-laws are now more aware and understanding of the challenges faced by working parents in this generation and they are usually very supportive.

Education has played a big part in broadening our horizons; the more educated we are, the broader minded we become.

The world has become a much smaller place. With more and more people travelling around, it's important for us to learn to respect new cultures, learn new languages, try out new foods, make new friends. When our children observe us accepting new situations as educational opportunities, they will find adapting to life's changes much easier. You will also be teaching by example that they can continue to cherish their own culture and upbringing, while learning about and appreciating new cultures as well as surroundings.

We care for our children out of a deep and unconditional love, never out of mere duty or obligation. Why not teach them the same principles as they grow? Wouldn't it be nicer if, once they're older and independent, they do things for you out of love and concern, and not from just a mere sense of duty or because it is expected by society?

My husband and I love being around family. We love spending time around our respective in-laws, cousins, and other relatives. We miss our extended family when they visit us and head back home or when we go back home having visited them. You feel a buzz when the whole family is together. Yes, of course, there are squabbles and banter but that is the fun of being part of a big family.

'It takes a village to raise a child'. When applied to the extended family, I find that the older relatives like grandparents, aunts and uncles can be valuable assets in helping mould your child to become what you want to see them be as an adult. Often, the child may even form close bonds with their extended family members and this emotional security can be a safe place for the child in unforeseen situations like an unexpected family break up or any other form of emotional turmoil.

Chapter 6

Baby steps

Early days

As we became pregnant in my mid-twenties, my husband and I had to learn the ropes through trial and error. Of course, as I said before, we both worked full time, we had a good friend circle and supportive family. However, finding out that you're expecting and the actual realisation of being pregnant are two different things. Many mums-to-be would agree the realisation doesn't sink in at the first sight of the blue strip on your pregnancy test. For me it didn't even sink in when I had an uncontrollable craving to eat spicy food at 4pm while at work. Nothing could satiate this craving! I couldn't wait to get home and persuade my husband to get me *Achari Ghosht* (Spicy Pickled Meat Curry). It was only during my 12-week scan, when I heard our baby's heartbeat for the first time and saw this tiny alien like peanut shaped creature on my scan picture.

Of course, the following months went by slowly at first, then flew past. Before I knew it I was perched on the bath tub, tiling the bathroom with my big tummy sticking out when I felt a contraction.

I was able to get maternity leave and get time to bond with our son after he was born. Our son was only breastfed while, later on, when our daughter came along she was breastfed and bottle fed simultaneously. This gave my husband an opportunity to bond with our daughter while I could catch up on some much-needed sleep!

What worked for me 90% of the time was having a consistent daily routine for the baby. Set time for waking up, set time for breakfast, play, lunch, and nap time. Evenings would follow with a good massage for the baby, bath, and dinner. I always incorporated a short reading session before putting baby to sleep. This might sound unusual for a baby, but research shows that reading to babies, even unborn babies, can have a dramatic effect on their mental, verbal, and emotional development.

I have to say, this has served me well over the years as both my children, now 17 and 11 have stuck to a similar routine. The reading habit that was instilled in them from infancy, continues with them even now. I am convinced that it helped them to speak earlier and more clearly, expand their vocabulary and become good readers from a young age. I cannot emphasise enough how important and beneficial reading to your child is, no matter how little they are.

After my daughter was born, I struggled to continue this bedtime routine with our son but I followed the advice of another wise person who suggested I get my then 6-year-old son to sit next to me with his book and read with him while I would be feeding my daughter. This worked out nicely and they both enjoyed reading not just to themselves but also to each other.

As my children grew older, I got them to read to me. Some of our most memorable and meaningful conversations, have been cuddled up in bed or the sofa, with the TV and gadgets turned off and having a good reading session or story time. Reading and discussing encourages dialogue and I have found that true with our son, who is at the tail end of his teenage years, and still doesn't hesitate to discuss his thoughts and feelings with us (as long as he excludes the cheeky tone that sometimes comes with it!)

Importance of a good routine

It can be a nightmare to get babies to sleep through the night. As usual you live and learn through trial and error with your first born. With my second baby, I shopped around and took advice from self-help books written by authors like Gina Ford and Dr Miriam Stoppard. I also spoke with other parents who had experiences similar to mine. It is totally inevitable for people to usually feel the need to offer advice incessantly as soon as they find out you're pregnant or are a new Mum. Whether it is old wives' tales or medical opinion or their own personal experiences, you will find no shortage of advice. Though I think it is always good to listen to a variety of ideas, just don't feel pressured to follow every single one of them!

For me what worked was trying out the advice and then adapting it to suit my own routine. For example, some said, 'You should put the baby to sleep in your bed,' others said, 'Baby should sleep in their own room, away from disturbance and light'. In the early months, I would have the baby sleep in a cot next to my bed. That way, I could get up and easily feed and/or change the baby's diapers in the middle of the night. I also put blackout blinds on the windows so that no streaks of light could seep through and wake baby up.

Parenting advice can be overwhelming. Some people may blurt out well-meaning comments like, 'Ah, the baby is not breastfeeding well, you need to top up with formula', 'Ah the baby is too skinny', 'Ah you are over feeding the baby, the baby is putting on too much weight'.

It's frustrating to think that having suffered 11 hours or more while in labour, you are still swollen and bleeding and bruised all over and people are telling you over and over again about everything that you're doing wrong with your baby.

I learned a tough lesson during that time, one that I still try and stick to when meeting new Mums, 'Never give your opinion or advice, unless you're asked for it'. You no doubt mean well, and you may think you are being helpful, but what it translates to a sleep-deprived, bruised and hormonally rushed new mother, is this, 'You can never do anything good enough,' 'You are useless,' 'You are not a good mother,' etc, etc.

At the same time, if you are a new Mum, if there is anything I have learned, is this: Give yourself a break. Don't let criticism bring you down. You have just brought this beautiful little human being into the world. Celebrate! Enjoy the bonding process! Do ask for help and if help is offered, take it!

Here are some practical tips for expectant and new Mums *and* Dads:

Mums

- Make sure you pack a hairbrush and lipstick in your hospital bag. You might need it for the post-delivery photos if you look anything as shattered as I did after my deliveries.
- Have some alone time with your immediate family, including your partner and your other children to welcome the new baby. Also include all other people who live in your home.
- Eat something you fancy. I enjoyed my favourite meal after my kids were born and my husband got me my favourite chocolates to keep my energy and sugar levels up.
- Don't worry if you're a bit tearful, the baby blues will be kicking in and hormones that were regulating your pregnancy will now be readjusting to help you start breastfeeding.

- Once you're home, spend some individual alone time daily with your other children (if you have any) without the baby. Just doing something simple such as reading a story together will reassure your older child of your love and attention.
- Above all, accept help or better still, ask for it. It could be something simple such as helping with laundry, taking your older kids out to the park, or just watching the baby while you take a nap.

Dads

- Attend all prenatal and antenatal appointments with your partner.
- Help pack the hospital bag! You will need to know where things are in case your wife is incapacitated at any time, which of course she is going to be. She is giving birth for crying out loud!
- Keep the tech charged up and movies downloaded on the phones, iPad, etc. You and your partner will need them to pass the time during initial stages of labour.
- Avoid work calls during labour, your wife will need your full attention, after all she is doing something far more important and productive than any of your colleagues could for you.
- Give her something bright and Cherrful. Jewellery helps (of course it does!), but her favourite flowers will raise her spirits just the same.

- Expect your wife to start feeling the effects of baby blues between day 1 and 4, and they can last a minimum of 1 week to 6 months. Remember, she is at a vulnerable stage and needs your reassurance and love. Keep an eye out for clinical depression which can sometimes be an after effect of pregnancy. Check with your doctors about symptoms to watch out for.
- It is great if you have family to help, but believe me, this is not an experience you would want to miss out yourself. Help with the baby during the day and take turns with night-time feeding and nappy changing. You will likely have a much happier baby and relaxed Mummy at home.

Chapter 7

Behaviour management

People in my line of work sometimes ask me, 'how do you manage a child's behaviour and deal with tantrums?'

I have put some careful thought into this answer, because everyone's way of dealing with a tantrum is different and there are so many different variants of dealing with tantrums in even a single culture, you run the risk of offending someone if you are not careful.

I know from my childhood, tantrums were not tolerated, shouting 'no!' to your parents or another grown up was out of the question at any age. Throwing your arms and legs in the air as if you are having a fit? I could never dream of getting away with it! If I did, the consequences could have been disastrous for me. Worst case scenarios would include a smack on the bottom for rude or disobedient behaviour.

That was then, this is now. I have also come across some parents, who claim not to smack their children, but for some reason they do not find anything wrong with screaming at them in a fit of rage, using the most deplorable language, sometimes even calling them despicable names. While in some cultures, many parents may feel justified smacking their child if the occasion (and offence) calls for it, I do not advocate any kind of physical or emotional punishment or discipline that is hurtful and damaging to your child. When I was younger and lived in India, you could get smacked or made to stand in the corner all day as punishment at school. I remember my horror of seeing a boy in class getting smacked. Thank goodness, those days seem to be long gone now.

'Because I said so!'

You may have read or even experienced, when your child was little, their favourite question, 'why?' I remember when reading to my children, each time we would come to the exciting climax of a story, my daughter would interrupt and ask, 'why Mum?' I would answer her and resume the story and that would be swiftly followed by another series of 'whys'.

My point?

Children are born with a most natural curiosity which leads them to explore their surroundings and make new discoveries about the world every day. It is natural for them to inquire and ask questions. As much as I'd love to dispel your fears – this doesn't get any better as they grow up. When our son was younger, I could easily get away with telling him, 'Because I said so!' Now, that doesn't seem to work just as effectively as before. He is now forming his own opinions and learning to reason. All too often I find myself debating with him as to why he should regularly polish his shoes or some such mundane task. It's like their debating skills get more refined as they go through puberty!

How often do you come across tired parents come home from a long day's work confronting a teenage child who's also had a disappointing day at school, getting involved in a verbal joust where each party gets entangled in words trying to get their points across? It makes sense to avoid confrontations until rest and refreshment or possible recreation has brought everyone into a more positive space.

Chapter 8

Discipline: Good or bad?

Does discipline always mean punishing your child or scolding them? *The Cambridge English Dictionary* describes the word discipline as 'training that makes people more willing to obey or more able to control themselves, often in the form of rules'.

So, one could argue that discipline has a positive aspect. Disciplining your child, would effectively mean training your child, right? How could you train your child to be obedient, to be kind, to be honest and hard working? Surely, with training comes consistency, correct?

To illustrate: (Heads up! I am not very green fingered but just stay with me here) Imagine trying to grow a beautiful and fragrant creeper like jasmine, in your garden or over your doorpost. The goal is for the plant to climb over your fence, adapt to the lumps and bumps of the wall and elegantly sweep over the door frame, forming a colourful and fragrant entrance. How do you train your plant to achieve this desired effect? It's never going to happen from day one. You need patience and – that word again – discipline! You need to support the plant with bamboo sticks. Also, you need to keep regularly manoeuvring the plant around the sticks to make sure they follow the desired path. As the plant grows, you will need to adjust the sticks or move them around, so your plant has room to grow while it is being supported. Why did I use this analogy? Our children can be compared to this beautiful and fragrant plant. They need support and they need to know their boundaries. They are also delicate and vulnerable so if you are too forceful or tyrannical, you run the risk of breaking their spirit. Too lenient and they will grow out of control. It is important that each family unit works together to figure out an appropriate balance that works – suits the needs of their children and their unique circumstances.

Self-discipline first

'*Do as I say and not as I do*!' is a rather well-known phrase. Ever had someone say that to you? If so, what did you think of that person? On second thoughts, I don't want to know!

The question we need to ask ourselves is, do I say this to my kids? Even if I don't spell it out verbally, do I convey that impression through my actions? For instance, do I teach my children that honesty is the best policy but if I am caught doing something dishonest, I try to wiggle my way out of it with a 'white lie'? Do I teach my child the dangers of munching on too much junk food but then I regularly hide and binge on that last sugary sweet in the fridge? Am I under the illusion that my children do not see through my words and actions?

Remember, actions speak louder than words. You can talk to them and teach them until the cows come home, but if you can't back up your words with your actions, you are entirely missing the point.

What if you are trying your best to set the best example through your actions but you slip up occasionally? Never be ashamed to own up to it in front of your child. You may think that your child will lose their respect if you have setbacks. Believe me, if you are honest with your child, they will respect you even more than before and you will be setting an example to honestly owning up to your mistakes.

Remember

- Discipline does not mean being harsh, tyrannical, or authoritative. Our children need loving guidance and need to know their boundaries.
- There is a strong link between positive discipline to nurture a happy family with relaxed parents and contented children.
- Positive discipline versus Negative discipline
- It is important, even crucial, to discipline ourselves first and then discipline our children.

Positive Discipline: 1–3 years olds

As you may have gathered by now, children in this age group tend to have shorter attention spans. They respond best to short and simple instructions and 'yes' and 'no' commands. Their brains are like sponges. They can absorb things around them very quickly. They begin to form words and sentences in efforts to talk. Toddlers also realise they can get your attention by using their voice and their arms and legs. They may have endearing gestures to express their delight or disagreement. Once they discover that they can throw their arms and legs around in a tantrum to get what they want, they keep trying that again and again.

So how do you manage temper tantrums? Dealing with temper tantrums at home is bad enough; dealing with them outside in full public view is even worse. I always go by the mantra, 'Forewarned is forearmed'. Hence, preparation is key in trying to manage or even prevent a tantrum. So how do you prepare to deal with a temper tantrum in two–three-year-olds?

My tips are the following:

- *Prepare your child* - Talk to your child about where you plan to go for the outing. If you're going to the supermarket, keep your young child engaged with conversations about the supermarket, such as, 'we are now going to get a trolley' or, 'we are going to the checkout now'. Preparing them for what to expect next is crucial to keeping their attention span which, let's face it – is never easy.

- *Keep 'em busy-* Keep little hands busy by giving them jobs to do like 'help mummy put the fruits in the trolley' or give them a piece of paper to 'tick' off the shopping list or have a handy little notebook and pen that they can draw pictures of fruits and stuff while sitting on the trolley. If you're a good multitasker, you can even use informal occasions as teaching opportunities to help them learn names of fruits and vegetables or other day-to-day items.
- *Think ahead-* Picture yourself in the following scenario: You're at the supermarket aisle and your child decides they have to have a packet of chocolate, (which was not on the shopping list by the way) and they don't plan on getting your permission. Your 'mummy senses' pick up the tell-tale signs of a tantrum brewing, the body stiffens, the face changes, their breathing becomes shallow and you fear embarrassing yourself by a loud spectacle about to be caused by this pint sized human: what do you do? Take simple, quick, and decisive action: Nip it in the bud straightaway with a firm 'no darling, we're not getting that now,' pick them up, turn around and distract them with something else. A simple, short, and sharp pre-emptive response like this prevents a full-blown meltdown of your child and puts you back in control of the situation. I can personally vouch for this, no matter how

many times I have come across this situation or have been presented with this problem with other children or my own. Using this technique time and again has served me and my clients well.

- *Get their attention* - If your child is slightly older and able to understand, try to speak to him *before* going out. Go down to his level, eye-to-eye, discuss with him in short and simple sentences the kind of behaviour you expect. You could say something like, 'Johnny, we are going to the shops now. Remember, what kind of behaviour does mummy want from you?' and then add, 'what kind of behaviour does mummy NOT want?' Do not settle for using phrases like 'good behaviour' or 'naughty behaviour'. Little Johnny does not fully understand the concepts of good behaviour or naughty behaviour! So, you need to specify in short: 'No screaming, no shouting, no kicking. If you kick, scream or shout, Mummy will not get you a treat at the end of shopping. '. And if they've behaved to your satisfaction, make sure you give them a treat *at the end* of your shopping. Let them choose whether it is an ice cream or a Happy meal, for example something you know they enjoy! A treat need not be foods only. It may be a pencil or a small notebook or a toy to complete their collection. Or a quick visit to an animal park nearby or a visit to a dear friend.
- *Say no to devices* - Avoid trying to use your phone

> or some other electronic device as a distraction for your child. The whole point of taking your child out to the grocery store is for him to learn about life outside the home. If you hand him your phone as a distraction, is he ever going to learn about what goes on outdoors? How can you expect him to learn to behave in the way you want him to, if his head is constantly down, eyes are constantly glued to a device? Are you opening his eyes to the wider world? Or are you just putting a literal screen in front of his eyes?

When I work with children in this age group, I follow the 'child led play' and 'learning through play' method. In this method, we encourage children to follow their interests and learn things such as verbal, written, sensory or motor skills. In using this method, you will find that even mundane chores can become an entertaining game for them, you are much more likely to hold their attention and get the desired results. For example, tidy up time can be turned into a counting competition or pretending to be a favourite character such as Cinderella or Superman. This can be an effective way to motivate young children to help around the home – to help clean or carry objects across the house.

Positive Discipline: children of 4 to 7 years

I find the ages 4-7 to be one of the most interesting years. A child during these years is more aware of his surroundings and is learning to respond to them. He has soaked up a lot of information in the first three years of his life and is now ready to 'reciprocate'. They tend to display confidence in their surroundings based on what they have learnt. Your four-year-old will be starting kindergarten. In addition to learning literacy, maths, along with other early childhood curricula, they will be learning to form friendships, getting along (or not!) with their peers at school. Children in this age group generally also *gravitate towards forming friendships with children* of the *same* gender. If positive discipline is managed properly, children in this age group yield loads of immediate and positive results in their development.

- Children in this age group tend to respond very well to immediate feedback. You might find that they will readily use polite forms of speech, such as 'please', 'thank you' and 'I'm sorry' etc. Use this to your advantage and reinforce these mannerly behaviours as often as you can.
- They will use plenty of imaginative play such as make-believe stories or characters, den building etc. and if you let them, they can stay busy with these activities for hours.
- They will also LOVE the outdoors. Encourage them to play outdoors as much as possible. Take them to the children's park and encourage them to jump, climb, skip, run, etc.
- You will find that if they do not get sufficient outdoor physical stimulation, they will be more

hyperactive and boisterous indoors. If you want them to learn to avoid using your living room furniture as a climbing frame, take them regularly to the parks!

Positive Discipline: Children ages 8 to 12 years

What is the best way to positively train your primary school age child? No longer a younger child and edging towards puberty, they may already be showing signs of calming down as their body gradually changes in response to the growth spurts. However, this is also the time when, as their bodies go through various changes, their hormones are starting to prepare them for their teenage years. You might find that their emotions can sometimes be a bit haywire, particularly as they start entering puberty. As the adult in the family, you can help your child understand these fluctuating emotions. During times like these, *you* need to be the stabilising factor. Try the following tips.

- Help prepare them for puberty with frank and open conversations of what to expect. Just talking with them once about the 'birds-and-bees' is never enough. Do not wait for them to approach you with questions; you need to use every opportunity to talk with them in a matter-of-fact way.
- Children in this age group start to get a better understanding of the world. Help them see the world around them through books and travel as

well as exposing them to various age-appropriate experiences.

- Don't shield them from the consequences of their actions, be it good or bad, help them experience 'cause and effect'.
- They may also become more self-conscious about their bodies and their growth, often comparing themselves with their peers. Help them to understand that 'everybody is different'. Their growth is unique to them. Sooner or later, everyone will transform from childhood to adolescence on their way to becoming adults. Help them to develop a positive view of their bodies as well as accept mood swings and confusion.

Positive Discipline: Teenagers and adolescents

How do you discipline or show consistency in your dealing with a pre-teen or teenager? Do not hold your breath; this may appear challenging. Yet as you go through this section you will find it is actually much simpler.

In all my training and experience in childcare and child psychology, one phrase is often repeated: Communicate with your child! Yes, we have talked about communication to establish a close relationship. This will come up again in this book but what does communicating with your pre-teen or teenager encompass?

- Talking to them?
- Listening to them?

- Teaching them?
- Shouting at them?
- Keeping quiet? (sometimes... let me explain why)

As a parent of an adolescent, you are still learning to understand this new emotional makeup of your child. You may think, "Oh well, my adolescent doesn't want me telling him/her what to do? I will embarrass them in front of their friends. Why should I bother?"

Your teenager needs you *now* more than ever. Why? Because they are at an age when they are no longer a child and don't feel the need to run to Mummy or Daddy with their problems. They are getting an understanding of their surroundings in the process of finding their own place in the world. As they grow older, they will undoubtedly want to spread their wings and they should be allowed to do so (within reason)! They will push their boundaries. They will want to take new risks that they wouldn't have thought of before. What do you do as a parent? Do you just turn them loose and leave them to their own devices? Or should you tighten the reins even more?

When your child was learning to ride their bike, did you provide them with training wheels attached to their bike or support them from behind as they wimbled and wobbled, trying to balance themselves on their bike? You didn't just buy them the bike and let them get on with it, did you? When you're supporting your child initially to help them balance themselves on the bike, you are effectively telling them,

'*We both are in this together.*'

'*I have your back and yes you may fall, but guess what, I am right here beside you, I will help you up*!'

You keep trying again and again and once they have mastered their balance, away they go!

Now apply this same principle metaphorically to your adolescent child. You are training them to be an adult. Yes, sometimes they need 'training wheels'. Quite possibly even a measure of intervention if they become overconfident and start to lose their balance.

Think about the following handy tips

- Help them to believe in themselves. Don't give them the feeling that they are inadequate or incompetent. They have just come into an age group where they may be getting more conscious of themselves either intellectually or physically in comparison with their peers. During their teenage years, these feelings of self-consciousness or inferiority complexes can get amplified to a much higher degree.
- Help them to stay humble. As proud parents, we always want to praise our children's achievements to others. If your child is exceptionally good at something, why should you hold back your commendation? They deserve the praise but a word of caution: Make sure it is genuine. I always remember a phrase, 'The higher they are, the harder they fall'. If you puff up your child's ego

too much, you run the risk of them becoming arrogant. Remember, we are trying to teach our children to keep growing and learning and not to have a 'know-it-all' attitude!

- Avoid unfair comparisons. Never compare them to your friends' or relatives' children. Your child has unique qualities and abilities that only they possess and nobody else can duplicate that. In fact, avoid comparing siblings as well.
- Keep going. As another very wise man told me and I tell this to all my clients, when it comes to training children and teenagers, 'DON'T GIVE UP and DON'T GIVE IN'. If you give up, they will likely give up as well. Not all children are naturally born with the drive to persevere towards a specific goal. If they see you give up in your endeavours, they will also find it easier to quit.
- Be their rock. While your children may not realise this when they are younger, they *need* you to be the parent. You need to be a stronghold, a rock for them to depend on. If you are uncertain about yourself or lack confidence in your own abilities, their confidence may be affected as well.
- Forgive yourself. More often than not, we want to do all of the above and most days we are raring to go. However, there may be times, when, as a parent, we do not do what we should have and that's ok. Remember, no matter whether this is your first child or your fifth, *you* are still growing

and learning as a parent. If you are going through a bad day, just remember, you *are* allowed one every now and again.

Chapter 9

A vital tool, not a threatening weapon

Communication is used by living creatures all over. Whether it is humans, animals, birds, fish, or insects, we are all designed with one common ability: To communicate in some form or another. Humans have the advantage of being able to communicate in verbal as well as non-verbal methods.

We can communicate in languages as well. If humans have this gift of being able to articulate their thoughts and processes across to another human being, can this gift also be misused?

I believe many of you out there will also feel this way because as much as I try to keep my cool there are occasional moments when I do lose it. The guilt that follows often leads you to painfully analyse the whole situation and then you ask yourself, 'what led to me losing my patience in the first place?'

I have since discovered steps you can take *not* to lose control even if you do lose your cool. Wait! Is that even possible? Yes, let me explain.

When your teenager does or says something that provokes you, you might be tempted to use the 'parent card' and shut them down on the spot. Or worse, you might lose your temper, start shouting at them, punish them or in other words, 'flex your parental muscle' to impose your authority on them. While you might think that worked when they were younger – you could quickly regain control of the situation. But is it still the best or most effective way to deal with this situation post-puberty? How about if you were to step back from the problem at hand, think about it and consider it from your teenager's point of view? You don't need to agree with everything they're saying or doing but 9 times out of 10 if you keep a cool head yourself, the situation will yield a better outcome. If you control your own reactions, instead of being dictated by your teenager's action, you would have retained control in that situation. Next time you are faced with a confrontation, consider the following suggestions.

Don't take it as a challenge to your authority!

Is my teenager/adolescent really trying to challenge my authority or are they curious to see how far can they fly? Could I should perhaps review some of the boundaries I've set for them in their childhood to give them some more room to grow and explore yet maintain essential boundaries? Growing up in India, it was always drummed into our heads, 'You must respect your elders', 'Obey your elders', 'Don't talk back'. For my own children I fully endorse these values.

However, there comes a time when we need to review a few important issues as they grow up. Of course, respecting your elders is still non-negotiable but what about other kinds of communication? While saying, 'Because, I said so!' may have worked perfectly well when the child was younger, it may not necessarily be in the best interests of either you or your children when they are adolescents.

Teenagers need more room to grow within the boundaries you've set for them from their childhood. However, if they are *never* allowed to express themselves or voice their heartfelt opinions (right or wrong) within a safe and mutually respectful environment, you may never get to know their inner personality. You may never be able to put right those 'wrong' opinions. Worse still, they may be tempted to put on one personality in front of you and another behind your back. Do we really want that?

Make an effort to get to know their friends.

You may have heard several sayings such as, 'show me your friends and I will tell you who *you* are' or 'birds of same feather flock together'. If you think that *we* are moulded by our surroundings, you will be surprised how much influence *our* kids imbibe from *their* peers. I always recommend that parents get to know their children's friends not just when they're little but especially when they're older. When you used to organise play dates or kids' parties when they were younger, it was great, but now that they have grown up a bit, they may prefer to organise or rather disorganise their 'play dates' themselves.

If you want to get to know your teenager, part of the process is to get to know their friends. Many parents I have come across tend to use one of two extremes. They ban their teenager's friends from coming inside the house at all, assuming that they're all a bad influence. The other extreme is they let them come and go as they please and let them spend hours and hours and hours unsupervised in your child's bedroom.

Both are polar opposites and neither of those extremes is ideal. If your child's friends are indeed as bad as you may think they are, should your child be associating with them even outside the family home? If they are harmless, is it still a good idea for them to be locked up together unsupervised in their rooms for hours on end?

Why not try a middle ground, ask your child to regularly invite their friends, one or two at a time, to join the family for a meal or for some joint activities or outings together. Doing this can help you get to know your child's friends without being too judgemental about them.

Spend time with your teenager.

It goes without saying that we are all living such busy lives what with work, household chores, family, and relatives etc., we are often too drained out to expend energy spending time with our adolescent. We talked about discipline not just playing a negative role.

There is also positive discipline. Part of this positive discipline aspect is that you regularly must take the time to communicate with your teenager. Go out for lunch once a week and catch up on things that are happening at school or with their friends, go for a game of bowling or for a walk and take the time to chill with them. Even activities such as spending time listening to their favourite genre of music or playing video games with them can be good opportunities to share their interests without coming across as overbearing.

Don't monopolise a conversation or start by scolding them about something. You want occasions like these to be refreshing for both your adolescent and you. Don't give them long lectures about their goals or grades every time your child opens up to you. If you're interested in finding out about how things are going at school, just ask them! Remember, this is a 'safe space' for your adolescent to share their deep thoughts and feelings. Even if they do not respond as openly as you'd like, don't give up.

You could start by mentioning how your day went or what upset you or pleased you about something.

When you regularly take the time to converse with your teenager even if it is just for short bursts of time like while driving to and from school, you are not just reaching their heart but are also helping mould them and voila! The positive discipline reigns!

Show interest in their interests.

Show interest in things that interest *them.* Why is this even more important when raising teenagers? As they hit puberty, you may find your son or daughter becoming a bit quieter and more thoughtful. It does not mean they are planning anything sinister! It just means that they are 'taking more in', they are thinking things over in their mind. Like me perhaps you too found when we were teenagers ourselves, we would often prefer to be left alone with our thoughts. It could be about anything that interested us.

The same goes now for your teenager. Ask them what interests them and make efforts to get to know their likes and dislikes. This is a good starting point to help you engage with them better. In my case, our son has recently shown a great interest in IT and programming languages. It seems, that this comes naturally to him. Even when he is quiet and in deep thought, it is usually because he is trying to solve a coding problem in his head. Now, for me to be able to meet him at his level, I need to make an effort to get some knowhow of his coding languages (which I am terrified of, by the way!). Fortunately for me, at moments where I *really* cannot understand his coding genius, I can sometimes get away with passing the buck to my husband who himself is an IT expert.

As long as there is one of you who can share or show a sincere interest in your teenager's interests, you will find it much easier to get to know them on a new level. The additional advantage is that, once your adolescent sees that you are making a genuine effort in sharing *their* passion, *they* will be much more likely to share *your* interests too.

Chapter 10

Provide physical and emotional stability

Over the years we have moved homes so many times; as a child, I moved from India to Europe, then to the UK and since getting married we have moved home multiple times, both before my kids were born as well as while they were growing up. Yes, there have been times when things were up in the air, your routine is so out of whack and you're having to make do with lovely leftovers or *khichdi* for dinner two nights in a row.

Throughout these changes, we always kept our family together, not just physically but also emotionally and mentally. What do I mean?

Well, more often than not, when you have major changes happening in your life whether it is to do with moving home, often from one city to the next, and from one school to another, having a baby, suffering bereavement, having visitors etc—the consistent routine you've established, gets temporarily interrupted. And that is fine and to be expected as part of life.

Happy interruptions to our daily lives add variety and flavour to life and it goes without saying that sad interruptions such as a bereavement or an illness can temporarily suck the joy out of life as well.

These are the things that make us resilient and adaptable. If you maintain your positive discipline, in the form of regular communication, which gives your kids the attention they deserve, you will find that they are better able to cope with other changes which may be out of their control.

Consider a few of the following practical pointers I have learned more through personal experiences than training.

- Try to keep changes to a minimum. If possible, try not to move homes and change their schools at the same time and vice versa. If for some reason you don't have a choice, plan your move carefully and well in advance to keep disruption to a minimum., eliminating them entirely if possible during exams.
- Let older children have their own room or at least their own space so that they can keep their thoughts together and get on with their interests while you're settling into your new situation. If they must share a room with a sibling, let them work out a rotation between them to take turns keeping their rooms in order.

- If you have visitors, avoid evacuating your child from their own rooms, especially when they have just settled into routine. Why? A child's room should be their haven of safety, something they have some measure of control over. It is never good for your child's mental well-being to be evacuated from their haven. If you don't have a guest room (which, let's face it, many don't) and your relatives or friends come to visit, consider offering up your own room instead.
- Whatever changes you go through, always keep communication open between you and your child, both individually and as a family. This will always provide your child with the emotional and physical stability they deserve and help weather whatever storms of change come their way.

Chapter 11

Resilience and adaptability

How do you encourage and train your child to be resilient as well as to adapt? Or do these qualities come naturally to some people and not to others?

To answer this question, why not do some soul searching ourselves? Are we naturally resilient to the ups and downs of life? Do we fret and fuss about changes we don't like? Over the past year or so, we have all experienced so many changes to our daily living.

When I started writing this book, the pandemic didn't exist but now we are all living in a 'new normal'. Consider the example of a typical day in the life of a modern working family in India, prior to the pandemic. Perhaps this might help paint a picture: You're used to having a domestic worker to do jobs around the home, the dusting, the daily sweeping and mopping, the washing up, the laundry, ironing, etc. Then, if you pay them extra, she would help with the cooking and cleaning up as well as babysitting duties. Mummy then had more time and energy to cook delicious food 2–3 times a day for the whole family.

If you were a working Mum, you could perhaps afford to pay for a fulltime domestic worker. When the pandemic hit, millions of households in India and around the world were put under strict lockdown. In fact, India's first lockdown in 2020 was widely referred to as the 'strictest lockdown of the world's largest democracy'. Unless domestic workers lived with the family, nobody could come to your house to work. Mums and Dads had to work from home, schools were closed and children started studying at home. Supermarkets around the world reduced their food supplies due to the lack of production and broken supply chains. We were all cooped up at home and no one was allowed outside, sometimes not even for a walk or for shopping. Days turned into weeks, into months and now, years have passed and we all have been trying to come to terms with aftereffects of the pandemic.

These have been unprecedented circumstances but what has the pandemic taught us? Humans can adapt. Perhaps by force if not by choice but nevertheless, we are resilient. Did we have to wait for a global pandemic before we took stock of our lives?

During the first lockdown, I remember reading an article talking about women doing the bulk of the domestic chores *in addition* to having to work from home and home school their children. It took a pandemic to inform people that women often end up carrying most of the family responsibilities.

Now, many of these sensitive husbands and well-meaning extended families including children have realised that they can also do their part in lightening the load of the working Mummy. How so?

I have put together a list for you that you may like to go through with your family.

- Get help—I don't mean waiting around for a miraculous offer of help to appear out of nowhere. Be proactive. Assign jobs to different family members. If you're cooking a meal, assign a family member to chop all vegetables, get the ingredients together and if possible, cook together. If you are doing laundry, ask someone to hang up the washing. In this department, I will give credit to my Dad and all the male relatives in my family. No matter their age, they've always ironed their own clothes and if you ask them nicely, they will even do *your*s with a smile! Cooking and household chores were never gender specific for them. And this is something I want our son to grow up learning.
- Take turns—One of the first social skills we learned as children in kindergarten was to take turns, whether it was while playing games or helping the teacher, we all had to learn to play

our parts according to our abilities. Even as we grew up and started working for a living, we worked our required shift and went back home. Taking turns or working 'shifts' is almost second nature to us. How about applying this principle to domestic chores? Is it *always* the mother's job to cater to the rest of the family's demands? Can we split housework equally between all the members so that everyone gets an equal amount of time to relax? Or do we need drastic turns of events to take place such as an unexpected illness or a broken limb before we can allow the mother of the house to put her feet up and rest? Remember, taking turns eases the pressure, lessons the burden, cheers up those involved and brings the family together.

- Everyone can play their part—As you may have gathered by now, my way of managing my family may not necessarily be the typical, traditional Indian style. However, I do feel privileged to be in an advantaged position. Why? Because, I have had the opportunity of living in multiple countries. Growing up, I had the opportunity to live with extended family both in India, Europe, and the UK. I have been able to observe the operations of numerous working families throughout my career.

In every circumstance, each family is different in

their approach to matters as no two environments are the same. What always helps is when each and every family member chips in to play their role to get proactively involved in the work needed by the family. Even younger children can contribute.

Regardless of whether you have external help or not, start by teaching them to clear up their toys when they finish playing. Surely, they can help to set the table for dinner or bring their plate to the sink to wash up. Older children can do other age-appropriate tasks such as wash the dishes or unload the dishwasher. They can help clean the toilets and sink, and keep their rooms tidy.

If you live within a joint family with elderly parents or in-laws, they can also play a role. They may have some physical limitations, but they could do other things like provide moral support and encouragement. They could help children with homework or read with them, tell them stories or even cheer you up with a cup of tea or coffee after a long day at work.

My then 80-year-old grandfather (although born and raised in a strict Indian family himself) always found himself getting up early in the mornings. Guess what tradition he started? Making morning tea for the whole family and wait for it... he would even deliver cups of tea to his son and daughter-in-law's bedroom each morning! This tradition he created is now being followed by his own children. Do you know why he loved doing that? In his own words, he 'wanted to be of use in his old age'. This was his way of showing gratitude to his children for caring for him. My Dad always insisted on cooking for us, his adult children, whenever he visited. Same with my Mum and mother-in-law, they both love whipping up their favourite meals for the family when we all pay them a visit.

The bottom line is no matter where you live, no matter your background, no matter who you live with, whether you have a large or small family, each member in the family can be resilient. This helps the whole family to adapt to changing circumstances.

Chapter 12

Yo-yo parenting

What is yo-yo parenting? This idea came to my mind one day when I was talking to one of my clients. They approached me with a problem: their child would throw tantrums if he didn't get his way. When Dad is not around and Mum tries to discipline the child, she isn't able to get through to the child. The child ignores her and does whatever he likes. After a lengthy discussion with the parents as well as observing the child, I came to understand the dynamics.

Dad has a very strict approach to things. He doesn't allow any screen time even for short periods, the child has to eat everything on his plate and cannot move a muscle until he does. Mum and Dad frequently disagree about parenting methods especially in front of the child.

On the other hand, Mum is overly lenient. She freely

allows her child to graze on snacks throughout the day instead of sitting down during mealtimes, the child is often allowed to stay up till late even on school nights and often falls asleep on the sofa well past midnight.

This lack of unity of thought about routine resulted in the child not knowing his boundaries. The child didn't know where he stood with either parent as they both have such different parenting methods. He had no structure to his daily routine.

This yo-yo parenting, going from one extreme method to another at such short intervals cannot be good for the child or the parents in the short and in the long terms. This leaves the door open to innumerable problems.

My tried and tested solution to this problem is simple. Be consistent! Why do I emphasise this?

Chapter 13

Consistency and routine

Why do you and your spouse need to be consistent in dealing with your child? Consider the following example.

Young Johnny asks his Mum for sweets before bed, to which his Mum says no, as his teeth would rot with the sugar. Now Johnny thinks for a minute and when Mum isn't looking, goes to ask his Dad the same question and his Dad, without looking up from his iPad says ok! What do you think goes through little Johnny's mind? 'I have a 'yes' answer and a 'no' answer. Which one should I choose? I'll go for the answer I like'. How likely is Johnny to try the same tactic next time? Fast forward a few years adding similar inconsistencies in Johnny's life.

Will these experiences lead him to be a strong, stable and single-minded individual? I doubt it.

Now consider the opposite result, Mum and Dad

are both on the same page that is, consistent with their responses. They already have explained to Johnny why it's a bad idea to have sweets before bedtime. Yes, he might end up in a small huff, but in the long run, would he be more likely to respect his Mum and Dad for not contradicting each other?

Establishing a good routine from earlier stages

From the time babies are born, they automatically form their own routine. They need feeding every 2–3 hours. In between they sleep, they wake up and need their nappy changed, feed to then go back to sleep again. This cycle goes on for the first few days until the baby is able to stay awake and alert longer for play time, which includes just stretching a little and looking around.

Even as we grow older, our bodies have their own unique body clock. It needs adjusting and readjusting according to our eating, waking and sleeping patterns. If you are unwell or when you travel across time zones, you notice your body clock goes out of sync. It needs to readjust to the change.

Your growing child needs a consistent routine. As your child is constantly growing, they need age-appropriate nourishment, mental and physical stimulation and rest. Of course, the younger they are the easier it is to train them into a routine. What do you do if you are in a situation like the earlier mentioned family? Is it too late? Is all hope lost? No!

Children naturally possess resilience and adaptability,

which sadly, often diminishes as they grow into adults. Resilience is both strength as well as flexibility. Along with adaptability, it enables children and adults—indeed all living creatures, to find the best path of practicality with comfort. Use these to your advantage. First, sit down with your spouse privately and jointly decide on the routine and parenting style you both wish for the family especially your child [and siblings, if any]. If you need to put these down in writing, so you both remember, even better! Next, sit down with your child (when they are old enough to understand) to explain the new house rules to them.

You don't need to be tyrannical. Just use simple language such as, 'We love you very much, we are sorry, but we have let things to get a little out of control, we are going to try to do better from now on and need your help with this'. Simple and honest acceptance like this can work wonders and your child's respect for you will grow. If your child is not old enough to understand, you will find that just going ahead and putting the agreed routine in place from the next day will work just fine.

Children thrive on routine. You need to work out a routine that fits your family life and stick with it.

Start on it and keep it going

I would emphasise one key point here. *Only start if you mean to carry it through*. There is no point in starting a routine if you both as parents do not intend to follow through on it. It would be like embarking on a journey and then constantly changing routes, left and right, backwards and forwards with your car. Can you imagine the chaos this would create? Won't this confuse you and your passengers as well as the others on the road? It won't help you reach your destination—rather it will make your journey more tiresome. Your passengers will become frustrated and stressed. In the end, nobody would be happy.

Chapter 14

Child rearing – whose responsibility?

Until recently, it was assumed that the women of the house, usually a wife and mother, would take on the responsibilities of childrearing as part of running the family home.

If you were a daughter-in-law living in a joint family, it was assumed that you would be responsible to cater to the needs and demands of the rest of the family members. This would include not just your husband, but also your parents in-law, any brothers or sisters-in-law as well as your own children. If you were fortunate enough to employ an '*aayah*' (nanny) you could count on that help, however more often than not, you were automatically expected to know the ropes from the day you got married.

This theme is still common in many rural households in India and is still glamorously featured as the backbone of many TV shows. With changing times, women are working shoulder-to-shoulder with their husbands, so much so, that the idea of stay-at-home mothers serving the immediate and extended family is getting more and more uncommon.

So, how do we deal with the changing times? Would it be correct to stick to the traditional somewhat old fashioned view that it is only the women who have the responsibility of rearing their children? I think not!

At the outset, I mentioned that the father is an equal contributor to the conception of a child. Also, in most countries around the world, especially in India, the child carries the name of the father on their birth certificate all the way through to adulthood. Consequently, would it then not make sense that the father is equally responsible (if not more) for the rearing and training of children?

What if you are a working mother trying to juggle both work and home responsibilities? Suppose you have an ideal family arrangement and you live within a joint family. Your parents-in-law or your parents, who live with you or live nearby, are incredibly supportive. They can readily help around the house whether it is with chores or with children. You love your job and do not have financial constraints. You and your husband have a loving marriage with no outside influences. In cases such as these, would you agree that the ultimate responsibility of running the household most often still falls on the woman of the house? Why is that?

My take on this is that, over the centuries, roles within

the family have been automatically designated and we have all found our comfort zones. Men had always been the ones to go out to work all day and bring home the bread and butter (or bacon); women on the other hand had been used to staying home and rearing the children.

Since the turn of this century however, especially after the First and Second World Wars, women have had to go out to work while the husbands were either away working abroad or sent to war for years on end. Women had to be inventive in managing the little money they had and working out ingenious ways of making ends meet. I guess that mentality seemed to have trickled down over the decades. Soon after the wars, countries realised that women now made up most of their workforce in the public sector services. They were not just organised but also productive while juggling their work and family responsibilities. These entrepreneurial women had also realised how liberating and fulfilling they found being able to use their skills in so many ways. Eventually, as economies grew, families realised that they are much better off financially having two incomes instead of scraping through with just one.

So, after having considered this history lesson through my lens, what conclusion can we draw? My conclusion is that in modern times it is commonplace, even necessary, for husbands and wives to both work to support the family. In addition to all the work and family responsibilities, childbirth and rearing, women also have emotional needs. While a working mother still plays an integral part in the smooth running of the family, now she also needs *more* love, support, understanding and appreciation from her family to help keep her mojo in fulfilling both her roles.

To work or not to work – that's the family question!

After having considered how fulfilling and necessary it can be for a Mum to be working to earn a living, do not be under any misconception that all women feel the need to go out to work in order to claim their identity or independence. I believe that each family is different. Certainly, each family's circumstances are unique. Therefore, the decision to work or not to work should not just be the burden of the woman to carry but should be decided jointly after considering the unique needs of each family.

You could consider some of the following five points.

- Do we need a second income?
- How will the children be cared for? Will they need to stay at home for long periods alone and unsupervised? Can a trusted family member help with childcare? Do you need to hire a trusted babysitter?
- Who will take care of household chores? Will the whole burden of cooking, cleaning, laundry, ironing, shopping, errands continue to fall on the shoulders of the mother? Or can family members pitch in and take up responsibility for some of the chores themselves?

- Will it be feasible to hire a domestic worker?
- Children aside, how will this affect your marriage? If you are managing childcare within the family by working opposite shifts to each other (Mum working during the day, Dad working at nights) will you regularly have quality time to spend with your spouse?

A range of factors come into play when both parents must go out to work. I have always worked throughout my adult life. I enjoy the feeling of being mentally stimulated outside of my family environment. I also find that working alongside caring for my family gives me a sense of fulfilment, a sense of achievement. However, in my quest of trying to find fulfilment, I admit I have sometimes struggled with trying to find the perfect work–life balance. I could never have dreamed of neglecting my kids or failing to provide for their basic needs. However, I found that, all too often, I would end up trying to juggle being the perfect working professional and a perfect mother and guess what, I couldn't be either! So, after much trial and error, I came to the following conclusion:

A perfect work-life balance does not exist, but a good work life balance can be achieved. How?

Consider some tips to help you juggle your work and family life.

- Keep work and family separate. The temptation is usually to bring your work home or try to juggle work and kids along with your spouse. However, it does *not* end well. You end up doing half a job at both things and being fully stressed while pleasing no one.

- If you must work from home, keep a designated area just for your work, whether it's a small room, a corner of your bedroom or living room and make that a no-go zone for your kids.
- Keep fixed work timings. Although, I admit I don't have this quite figured out as I tend to reply to work emails late at night or on weekends. Try not to check work emails outside business hours. If you do, you can't resist replying to them straightaway or you will stress over them until the following workday. Is it really worth it?
- Do not make or answer work calls during family time unless it is an emergency. In the long run, your children will grow to appreciate that you value family time and they also learn not to interrupt you during your working hours unless urgent.
- It is not a bad idea to sometimes let your kids see you busy during your working hours or trying to reach the occasional deadline. It teaches them the importance and rewards of hard work, accountability and time management and will hold them in good stead when they're older.
- Now that you have decided that you can manage your work-life comfortably and the extra income

in the bank also doesn't hurt, what can you do to make the transition smoother? Don't forget, resuming work after your maternity leave or even going from a stay-at-home Mum to a working Mum requires some adjustment for the whole family. So, how can you bring about this transition in a way that is hassle-free and comfortable?

Have a look at these suggestions. I have found them to be useful in many areas relevant to a healthy work-life balance.

- **Communicate!** (Yes, that word again!)
  Discussing matters before hand with your spouse makes a huge difference. Do not hesitate to explain what is in your mind but be prepared to also listen to the viewpoint of your spouse. Choose your time of communication wisely. It would be useless, if you're trying to discuss something important with your spouse while you or they're rushing through a deadline. The message would not go through and you will both end up stressed. Instead, discuss your plans in a calm atmosphere, when the children are in bed and when you both are relaxed. *Caution*: Don't use your children as 'go-betweens'. Ever heard of Chinese whispers?
- **Set your priorities and plan ahead!**
  Some people don't mind having a 'get-up and go' attitude for everything in life. However, I find it

easier to plan ahead and take things step-by-step, starting with the most important task at hand and working my way down to the least important. Sometimes, I admit I tend to get distracted, but I have to remind myself to stick to the priority list. That way even if I haven't got all the jobs done at the end of the day, at least I'll have got all the important ones done.

- **Be a good time keeper**
  Although my own family hasn't been entire successful in this yet, but I have seen the benefits of keeping time, especially when your plan includes others. Never give someone a time if you have no intention of keeping it. Remember that others' time is as precious as yours and they lead busy lives too. The same goes for your spouse and children. If you are expected somewhere at a certain time, do your best to stick to it. More importantly, ensure that you do not end up with a nickname behind your back, 'Mr and Mrs Tardy'!
- **Be flexible**
  You can organise your life all you want, but if you do not allow room for some flexibility, things can become stressful and frustrating. I have had to learn this, especially when dealing with secular authorities or travel arrangements in India. It is better to plan ahead but also to prepare for eventualities such as government holidays,

unexpected closures, road traffic etc.

- **Be gracious with each other**:
Do you keep finding fault with your spouse for leaving the kitchen messy after cooking a meal or your child for not clearing up their toys? I do but I remind myself that my spouse did think of cooking a dinner on days when I needed time off in the evening. There were some extra dishes in the sink, but hey, all I have to do is load up the dishwasher, right? My child has left her toys scattered on the floor and that's an opportunity for me to be thankful that at least she isn't glued to a screen, instead she is using creativity in playing with her dolls and teddies. Sure, I'll remind her to put away her toys once she's done with them but until then, why not enjoy the moment? Or better still, join her in her imaginative game! Instead of being upset over the 'small stuff', why don't you sit back, put your feet up and enjoy a cup of tea or if you prefer, a glass of wine.
- **Have a trustworthy friend you can talk to**
I am not talking about any old gossip girl kind of friend. I am talking about a good, sensible friend who will listen to you in confidence and understand you. This person needs to be someone who knows you, your background and your family. Someone who will not just tell you what you *want* to hear but what you *need* to hear even though sometimes you may not agree.

Friends who genuinely care for you are not fair-weather friends. They are all-weather friends, they are there for you for the good, the bad and the ugly.

Chapter 15

Teaching them to be polite and well-mannered

What are manners? There is an old English saying, 'Manners maketh the man'. This almost defines us both as individuals as well as civilised people. Isn't that true in so many cases? When you think about it, our manners say a great deal about us. I have narrowed manners down to two quite simple categories:

- Verbal Etiquette
- Non-Verbal Etiquette

Let's consider the verbal etiquette first.

Is verbal etiquette simply limited to the habitual use of words such as 'Please', 'Thank you', 'Sorry' and 'Excuse me'? Of course, these are important in conversation.

I remember always being told to mind my 'p's and 'q's, in other words, 'please' and 'thank yous', especially when speaking to my elders. Does that mean only children need to be polite and mannerly? What about when we speak to family members? Time and again you hear in movies, slug lines such as, 'Friendship mein "Sorry" ya "Thank you" nahin bolte' (You don't say 'please' and 'thank you' in friendships)

During my visits to India, I often get the impression that well-meaning family or friends almost discourage you from being polite or showing your gratitude. They feel you are being formal. I remember yet another childhood lesson that was emphasised so much in our family, 'charity begins at home'. If we are not kind and gracious to our children, can we expect them to turn out to be the same? Does saying, 'please' and 'thank you' or 'sorry' somehow belittle us as grown-ups in front of our children?

To illustrate, I remember once when I was a child, maybe 5 or 6 years old, I used to love watching a cartoon video. One day, to my utter disappointment, I realised that someone had made a recording over the video. It was my uncle who didn't know that was my favourite video. Nevertheless, he sincerely apologised to me after he found out. My respect for him grew to be more than my love for that video.

Do not hesitate to be sincere and gracious to your children. They will love and respect you even more for the fine example you are setting before them. Yes, I am still guilty of scolding my children for some unexplained mischief I've come across only to realise later that they had nothing to do with it. Should I just let my pride come in the way or should I avoid the subject with my kids to pretend nothing went wrong or should I skim over it to justify my actions?

I think you get the point; I should simply apologise. Never hurts to say, 'Look, I'm really sorry. I didn't realise that. I'll try to be more understanding next time.' I've had to use those words with our son when I misjudged him. I was happily surprised by his response; he gave me a hug and he said, 'It's ok Mum, don't worry'.

Verbal etiquette involves teaching ourselves along with our children to use those 'polite' words. They also refer to our demeanour, how we carry ourselves, how we honour people around us, and how we define our attitude towards children. Essentially, how we treat people around us. When we are polite, our children will follow these habits.

What about the other form of politeness and manners, such as non-verbal etiquette?

You might wonder, 'what on earth does she mean by non-verbal etiquette'? Is that even a thing?

Well actually, yes, it is!

Imagine you're going for a walk and you see an elderly gentleman or a pregnant lady struggling to carry their grocery shopping. Or you're in a bus and you see an elderly lady struggling to stand when you're comfortably seated. In both scenarios, you note that there are other people around but they are all either oblivious to the situation or simply do not care at all. What would you do?

Perhaps, your conscience might prick you into getting up and offering your own seat or to help that elderly gentleman with his shopping. Perhaps you wonder, 'if I reach out to offer help, they might misunderstand me and misjudge me' or 'just let them be, they'll survive'.

We know now that society is busier now and life is faster paced than ever before. Often we can't be bothered to extract ourselves from our phone screens to notice these opportunities to help people in front of us. You might ask, 'if I don't offer to help, I am sure someone else will!' But guess what? The other person is likely thinking the same thing!

What is the point of this exercise? The point is to remind ourselves that we are trying to raise our children to be polite and well-mannered members of society. Yes, this begins with us! *We* notice that elderly gentleman or that pregnant lady, *we* notice that elderly lady standing in the bus.

Now the onus is on *us* to be polite and well mannered. When our children notice *us* being polite and kind in *action, they* will be much more likely to also display that kindness themselves.

Now how about displaying this kind of non-verbal etiquette within our family? Recently, one of my parent clients asked me this question. She wondered how we can encourage our children to be polite and kind at home within the family?

She gave me a scenario: Her elder son never got along with his younger sister and they would always quibble and quarrel over small things as most children do. They were not very young children but they always would quibble about taking each other's stuff. At times, there would even be name-calling and shouting matches between them.

Things came to a head one day when, in frustration, they both started physically attacking each other, pushing and shoving each other, hitting and kicking one another. The mother tried to intervene, but by then the damage was already done. Both children had not only lost control of themselves, but they had embarrassed themselves as well as their parents because their neighbours saw the fight unfold.

After listening to the matter at length and trying to gather as much information as I could from the parents, my next port of call was to speak to the children individually. After our one-on-one discussions, I put together my understanding of the situation. It was time to have another meeting with the parents privately. I explained to them that sadly the problem seemed to stem from issues other than the children themselves. The children appear frustrated, not just with each other, but also with the family situation in general.

You see, there appeared to be no emotional connection between the parents and children. The children often felt that their parents would shrug off issues that they were struggling with at school such as bullying. The home environment was also very tense, the father often ignored them and they spent hardly any time together as a family.

The daughter also had valid concerns that her brother often could get away with what he wanted. She gave examples of instances when he was regularly cruel to her. As a younger sister, she complained she was expected to 'respect' her big brother in every situation. Her parents would not ever correct him. I had to draw this to the parents' attention because allowing this to continue would be in no one's interest. They agreed that there was work to do and that they needed to fix the basics.

I advised them that a good start would be to sit down with their children and have a heart-to-heart conversation and openly admit their failings. This would then encourage their children to open up and share their feelings too. Whatever steps they need to take would depend on how honest everyone is about their own mistakes in particular, and lack of kindness in general in the family. This would be a good starting point to improve the situation.

When children see that Mum and Dad are only human, that they also make mistakes sometimes and need love and forgiveness just like anyone else, children become more understanding, sensitive and empathetic to each other within the family as well as the community

After frequent reviews with the family, I am happy to report that they have become so much closer and kinder to each other. In fact, they are now a model family in their neighbourhood.

Points to remember.

- Never try to justify or make lame excuses for your

mistakes. Children may be inexperienced, but they are not stupid. They will easily see through any hypocrisy.

- Want to get good behaviour reports from school? Teach them good behaviour at home. The school's primary role is to provide academic education not just to train your child to be well-mannered. You must teach them to be polite and kind at home.
- Look for opportunities to commend and thank your child. No matter how small the action, your commendation will encourage them. Even if she brings you a glass of water, thank her for that. After all, being gracious and well-mannered are not just formalities, these are life skills that you are teaching your children and the point here is to lead by example.
- If you have a son, teach him to be a gentleman from infancy. Teach your son that being macho does not mean being mean or domineering; everyone should be kind and sensitive. Being sensitive does not mean being soft or being a push-over. It means that you are strong, yet kind and considerate towards others.
- Get your children involved in housework. You don't want them to grow up to be lazy, getting used to being waited on hand and foot by you or by a domestic worker? Our son has to tidy his room, take out the rubbish, vacuum and clear

up the table after meals. My daughter must help him. As a reward they both get appreciation. They might even get extra pocket money toward something special, provided they do their chores without prompting.

Our son also helps his Dad to cook sometimes and my daughter helps me bake cakes or make '*rotis*'. You are not just teaching your children to be self-sufficient. This way they learn not to take things for granted. At the same time, you're communicating with them and developing your relationship with them.

Giving them what they need

Over the years, India has become more cosmopolitan and Western businesses are making India one of the biggest commercial hubs in Southeast Asia. It is encouraging to see how progressive India's infrastructure has become over the years, although one cannot overlook the unending growth of 'new money'. People tend to have much more buying power and they can afford more and sustain a higher standard of life, earlier accessible only to the rich and famous.

The current trend in India is very much about brands and getting the best that money can buy. Affluent, modern India has become consumed with branded products and designer-wear even when we cannot afford them. By going beyond our budget to indulge our children's requests, surely, we run the risk of inadvertently teaching our child an 'entitlement' mentality.

Have you ever been to a fancy shopping mall in one of the big cities? You're patiently standing in a queue at the checkout and you suddenly hear a lot of whining and wailing. You turn around to look and you see a typical scene of a six- or seven-year-old-child throwing his arms and legs in the air. His parents are trying to control him.

For a second you worry that he is having an epileptic fit and then you realise, oh, he's throwing a tantrum because he wants his parents to buy something and they said no. Dad or Mom lose their cool to shout or possibly smack the child.

In all this melodrama, you also overhear a part of a conversation of a teenage girl with her Mum, 'Mummy, *mujhe yeh bhi chahiye, mujhe woh bhi lena hai*' (I want to buy this as well, I want that as well), Mum is trying to count her money but then resorts to using her credit card to buy what her daughter fancies. The end result is that the parents then have to work extra-long hours to pay for their children's demands and credit card bills, staying away from their home and children. It is a vicious circle. This is a scene I've come across several times. It saddens my heart to think that sometimes, parents are forced to buy something that they can't really afford to satisfy their children's whims or fancies. .

I want the best for my children too. If we can afford the best, we will give them the best whether it is in food, clothing, education, entertainment, holidays, etc.

We are functioning at an extreme though. Without realising, we've been teaching our children that they can have anything they want and expect their parents or others to foot the bill for all their whims and fancies. Are we so afraid to, sometimes, say no?

Our son once asked me, 'Mum, I'm bored with my iPhone 6 Plus. My friend has the latest iPhone, why can't I get the iPhone X?'

I had to think carefully before answering. I asked him, "Well, son. Your friends' parents can afford it. They both work long hours and can pay for it so that's up to them, we can't afford it right now and if you had a choice, what would you prefer: Mum and Dad away from home working longer hours but giving you all the latest gadgets and gizmos? Is it a good idea that Mum and Dad work enough that we can live contentedly yet still spend time with you every day?' Admittedly, he was crazy about the latest iPhone but his answer showed how mature he was. He said, 'We'd prefer spending more time with you and Dad.'

That's when it dawned on me, you can give your child all the luxuries in life, but if you don't give them the best of your time and teach them values, everything else doesn't really matter.

Chapter 16

Safety first – always

Physical safety

It's common to hear of all sorts of disturbing reports about children getting hurt or exploited and your weapon to protect your child will be, first and foremost, open communication.

Talk to them about keeping themselves safe right from a very young age. I was fortunate that I was able to work from home and spend time with my kids until they were ready to go to nursery school. I decided that they would only go to nursery once they were old enough to tell me all about it. And it worked well for me.

My way of preparing them to keep them safe include these pointers:

- Talk to them regularly about 'stranger danger'. Remind them every time they leave the home not to talk to strangers, not accept sweets or gifts from anyone they don't know. Repetition is key!

- Explain to them about their 'bubble'. We use the term 'bubble' to describe the immediate physical vicinity of the child. They do not need to let someone come into their 'bubble' if they don't like it. This gives the child some confidence and control over who they are comfortable with being around as well as anyone they would like to avoid for any physical contact.
- Explain the 'step back' technique. If someone comes to hug or kiss them and if they don't feel comfortable, they should step back without the fear of getting scolded.
- Talk to them specifically about anyone coming near their 'privates'. No one, not even any adult they know or trust such as a relative or even a friend should be allowed to do that. Allow them a measure of privacy when changing or using the toilet. Teach them to enforce that privacy themselves if you're not around such as at school or at a relative or friend's house.
- Look out for physical signs especially after they have been somewhere out of your sight. Signs can include, withdrawal, loss of appetite, touching themselves inappropriately or even saying something unusual or uncomfortable. Keep an eye out for anything they say that may signal that they are upset about something.

- If you decide for one reason or another, to send your child or infant to an external childcare facility, *always* make sure the place you select is rigorously checked and vetted. Look for excellent references and reviews and don't forget – trust your gut feeling.

I don't want to sound crude or worry you, but we are living in times when perpetrators will spare no expense in taking advantage of our young children. As parents, it is our duty to protect them from harm when they can't do this all by themselves. This is the way we can train our young ones to protect themselves when they're older.

Emotional safety

When they talk, listen – really listen!

It's easy to become distracted especially if their stories are lengthy or repetitive and you may find yourself switching off, picking up the phone and scrolling down social media. Catching up with your 'friends' or 'followers' on social media can be scheduled into your 'me-time' when the children aren't around, so stay away from the phone when your children are sitting with you.

When they reach their turbulent teenage years, they tend to become more withdrawn and start spending more time in their own world.

Even the most chatty and talkative child after having been articulate for the first 10 years of life can start responding to you in 'grunt' answers. You end up trying to read between the lines. You wonder, what happened to 'my sweet, chatty baby who used to tell me everything'? This sudden, almost overnight, change affects many adolescents. It is not because they have something to hide or don't want to talk to you but because they are learning to be more observant, taking stock of things around them and trying to find their own place to fit in.

They may also become more conscious of their changing bodies, often the arms and legs are not always in proportion to the rest of their bodies, but they don't want to tell you! Or their skin is breaking out or that they have infatuations.

Talk to them. As a loving and caring parent, you want to know how your child or adolescent is getting on during their day whether at school or play. They may not want to share their worries or concerns with you. Why not? Before asking them, ask yourself: Do I shut them down before they can finish what they're saying? Do I come across as paranoid or suspicious of them? Do I lecture them about right and wrong before they can tell me about their choices? Children have good instincts, they can sense when someone is interested in them. The person most interested in them should be *you,* the parent, rather than their peers.

Encourage them to talk and listen.

I know I talked about the importance of communicating much earlier, however this time, I want to talk about *teaching your children* to communicate. What do I mean by that?

Well sure, when they start speaking, they come out with these cute first words which we never forget. In my case, both my kids first words started with 'Dad' first, much to my annoyance!

But no, I am talking about teaching children to share their experiences with you. For example, when they come home from school or going with their friends on an outing, ask them how their day went, any activities they enjoyed as well as anything they didn't like.

Make it a habit to have daily conversations with them by sharing your day's experiences as well. Why is this so important?

You're encouraging them to open up, to talk about things they liked or disliked in their day. Doing so opens a window into their little minds about what they are thinking and feeling. This interactive communication is especially important, because you are teaching them the art of conversation and to express themselves in a safe environment without running the risk of feeling misunderstood.

In my line of work, you can always tell if a child has had many communication opportunities in their surroundings, at school or at home. Always communicate with your child starting from when they're infants. This will work well for the whole family when they're older and need (but may not always want) your input and guidance.

Chapter 17

Changing as they grow up

What do you do when your sweet little rosy cheeked child has transformed overnight into a spotty and grumpy teenager? Years ago, you went through these changes yourself. Now you might notice these changes in your adolescent even before they do. How can you help your child to overcome these challenges?

They may seem insignificant to you – however they are not! Certainly, this time of transition, of changes in their body as well as in their mindsets – is not insignificant to your child.

If you have not talked with them and prepared them to know what to expect, this phase can be very distressing for them. Whether it is your daughter having her first period or your son going through puberty while his voice and body shape changes *you* will need to extend

your full and unconditional support. If you wait too long for preparing them for these changes, you may find that they have already picked up inaccurate and often 'slang' information from their peers at school or among neighbours and relatives.

The key is to prepare them beforehand. It is never too early to start teaching them about their bodies. Even when your child is a baby, you could start with something quite simple such as helping them name their body parts during bath time. Age appropriate and matter of fact information should be given to the child. This continued interaction will help them understand that their body is an amazing gift and needs to be taken care of, so they are not needlessly embarrassed or ashamed.

Often the embarrassment comes when they become conscious of themselves. It is most natural to start comparing themselves to their peers. The bodily changes they start to experience are generally caused by hormone changes that they experience before and during puberty. This is a middle phase towards growing up where they are not really little children anymore but not yet adults either.

You may find that girls often reach puberty sooner than boys and may start showing signs as early as 9. On the other hand, some late bloomers may not show all the signs until they reach 15 or 16. Although some boys may reach puberty by the time they are 11 or 12, they often don't shoot up in height until they're in their mid-teens.

All these differences mean that everyone is unique and no one person has the exact same

physical or emotional makeup. We need to help our children to understand that they are unique but not different from their peers. Just like every plant takes its own time to grow and blossom, the same goes for our young ones.

Chapter 18

Friendly mother and motherly friend?

If you have had the pleasure and privilege of growing up with both parents nearby throughout your childhood and adulthood, what relationship did you have with your Mum? Was she a working Mum or a stay-at-home Mum? Did she cook you your favourite food several times a week? Did she have your favourite afterschool snack ready, the famous 2-minute noodles? Did she stay up with you bringing you hot cups of chocolate milk while you studied for your finals? Was she your friend or your parent? Or both?

As mothers we fulfil so many roles for our children. We give birth to them, we feed them, we get rid of the 'boo-boos', we take them to their first day at school, we teach them at home, we cook, we clean, we go through countless sleepless nights when they're sick, we attend parent-teacher meetings, the list goes on. So, what would you call the role?

Friendly mother

So, you see, when our kids are younger, they are so dependent on us. They need us every day – morning, afternoon, and night. Some need their Mummies more than anyone else. We are their superheroes. We wipe their noses, their mouths, their bottoms, all without blinking an eye. We understand their baby 'babble' when no one else can. Mums know all the names and dialogues of all their favourite movie characters. We can top and tail them, feed them, vacuum the house, wash the laundry, attend to work calls and cook a meal, often all at once! Any time of the day, we are there no matter what, with a tissue, with a cuddle, with a snack.

Wouldn't you agree?

Motherly Friend

Do you find, however, that when they grow older and perhaps get into their teenage years and they get a bit more independent, they don't want their mummies as much as before? Is this something that we need to take offense to or be disappointed about? After all, we have nurtured them throughout their childhood and attended to their every need. Do they not need us anymore now that they are spotty or beardy and all grown up?

There may be times when you feel that way, but I would not rush to that conclusion. Why? Well, think about the following pointers:

- Keep your emotional bonds close. Don't forget, if you've already worked hard at developing a close bond with them in their childhood, you will find that it's easier to keep that going as they grow older. Sure, they may at times be selective in how much they share with you at that particular moment but don't worry. If you give them some time, they will eventually open up to tell you the rest. Have conversations, not interrogations. After all, you are their parent friend, not their parole officer!
- Don't be suspicious or paranoid. When your child was younger, they probably used to run up to you after school every day and tell you everything that happened, all the tiny bits of information that they couldn't go without sharing with you. How should you adapt to this new behavioural change, when they are more reflective and less talkative?

  It might sometimes feel disappointing or even hurtful if you feel they're giving you a cold shoulder. However, that's usually not the case. In addition to bodily changes, they are also experiencing hormonal ups and downs and for some teenagers, this can be particularly challenging.

  As nurturing mothers, we mean well but to our hormonal teenagers, we may come across as overwhelming or smothering. Sometimes, just giving them a bit of space can be all they need. The last thing they need when they are going through their low moods is for us to bombard them with lectures, demands or complaints. Let them have some down time. You might be pleasantly surprised to notice how refreshed they feel after some quiet time and they will be more likely to respond favourably.

- Be their friend. This is one of those catch phrases that you might have heard before as well. Yes! It's as simple as that. As they grow older you may find that they will need you to be a friend more often than be a parent. However, don't forget that underneath, you are still their parent, and they will undoubtedly need their parent to be their anchor in times of difficulties.

Chapter 19

Social media and smart phones

Make them smart phone as well as social media savvy. No, I am not implying that you need to major in mobile phone technology or social media studies; in fact, your teenager probably knows more than you, like our son loves to remind me. Still, do you want to know my response? 'Yes son, you do know more about them than I do, but guess what, I know more about life than you do!' Are you interested to find out what your teenager has been up to on their texts or social media? Should you be? Absolutely! I am a firm believer in keeping a check on your children's activities. When they were younger, I *had* to know where they were and who they were with, *at all times*. I'm sure you did too.

Now that your children are a bit older and perhaps have their own phones, should you still be interested in knowing where they are, what they are up to on their phones, what they have posted online?

Well, think of it this way: just because you have allowed your teenage son or daughter to use a phone or access a social media account, does that automatically make them sensible enough to use these privileges responsibly and deal with the issues that come with it? Consider my use of the word 'privilege', something I keep reminding my teenage son. He is regularly reminded that having a phone or a social media account isn't a right or a necessity, it *is* a privilege. My husband loves to remind our children, 'Privileges can be given but can also be taken away.' Would you allow random people from all over, take a peek into your living room or worse, your teenagers bedroom anytime they wanted? Probably never. Would you allow your teenage son or daughter, with or without a friend, to wander around aimlessly and unsupervised in an unfamiliar and potentially dangerous neighbourhood where roughly 2 out of 5 people may potentially be thugs, gangsters or other predators? *Never*!

I know these are dark analogies but there are some similarities between the unfamiliar and dangerous physical world and virtual world. If you're not careful, unmonitored social media content and internet access can lead to high-risk situations.

Before you allow them to have a smart phone, talk to them about the uses and dangers of having a phone or a social media account. 'It's just a phone! What dangers can it pose?' you might ask? While I know it's essential to have a smart phone now, yet the dangers are abundant. We will come to that, but first, consider some of the *benefits* of training them to use a smart phone.

- You can reach them, and they can reach you at any time, giving you some peace of mind when they go out with friends.
- If used wisely, smart phones can be useful for schoolwork, learning skills, listening to music, getting directions to places.
- There is an abundance of reading and research material online.
- They can stay in touch with friends and family.
- It is a useful tool to learn and manage responsibility such as staying within their data and call allowance. Now let's consider some of the dreadful yet quite possible *threats*.
- They can become a target for thieves, be it actual thieves or cybercriminals.
- In addition to accurate and good information, they can be influenced by misinformation and fake news.
- They run the risk of being targets of online bullying, sexting, pornography and other forms of exploitation, either on the receiving end or even perpetuating (by sharing that is forwarding) it to someone else.
- They may occasionally get in trouble with the authorities in school or college if they use their phone without permission.

- They may inadvertently expose their personal details such as where they live, where they study, disclose to opportunists when they are not at home etc.
- If they upload their own pictures or pictures of other people without their permission, they may land themselves or others in legal problems etc and the uploaded photos may also end up being misused by people they do not know.

I realise that the list above does sound very worrying, and you may draw the conclusion that based on the potentially dangerous risks, you may not want your older children using a smart phone or social media. However, remember this: We are trying to move with the times here and adapt our parenting methods to the needs of our children. We are also trying to train and prepare our children to be responsible adults in society and this includes not wrapping them up in cotton wool until they get a 'culture shock' when they are older.

'If you prepare for the worst scenario in life, it may never happen.'

As much as we want to, we will never be there to protect our children forever from every single danger or disappointment in life, but we can prepare them and make them strong enough to be able to deal with unexpected challenges *should* they ever arise.

Phone privacy

Should you sneak up on their phones and look at all their text messages and calls etc?

Should you call up their friends (particularly ones you know) and enquire about the latest happenings?

We do need to be in-the-know about their personal matters, but can you only do so by prying behind their back?

If you feel you have valid reasons for concern, why not talk to them about it? Instead of sneaking up behind their backs, why not casually ask them for their phone and then check their messages *in front of them*?

Case scenario: One parent presented her concerns to me about what her fourteen year old was accessing on his phone but that she worried he would never agree to give them access to his phones and emails. She feared he would retort that 'it's his phone and it's his privacy'. My reasoning was this, 'Ok fine, you are entitled to *feel* possessive about your phone and perhaps you do not have anything to hide, but then as your parent, I am accountable for everything that you, as a minor, do and not do and I need to make sure that I know what I will be accountable for, so for all our sakes it's best that we go through your phone together. Period.' The parent used this reasoning with her teenager and she didn't have to explain her concerns to him again.

As parents, we remain accountable for what our children get up to, on-line and off-line. When teenagers understand that their actions, reactions or responses can have ripple effects on the rest of the family, particularly on their parents, they are more likely to cooperate.

Chapter 20

Eating habits and exercise

You are what you eat.

It is true, isn't it? Whatever we eat, whatever goes in our bodies basically becomes part of us before finding its way out.

We want to teach our children about healthy eating habits, about different foods out there and give them a good variety of options to enjoy.

Perhaps many of you are vegetarians or vegans. Many are non- vegetarians. Some are fruitarians, some are pescatarians, some are vegetarians but eat eggs and dairy products, some are completely vegan. Whatever your diet preference, it goes without saying, that you will have plenty of options in your chosen food groups.

Coming from India, I know that food plays a huge role in our lives. We love to talk about it, share recipes and obsess over Instagram food pictures. It is part of who we are; it reflects our beliefs, our upbringing, our health preference and even the part of the country we belong to. I love food and everyone in my family is a foodie, no questions asked. Given the chance, we could talk about food all day long. We love to try different cuisines and different styles of cooking. The spices of India are not just famous worldwide now but are legendary from ancient times.

We all have our favourite street foods. Often some of these street vendors sell freshly cooked food which, in my humble opinion, is tastier than some 5 star restaurants.

When you put food and self-discipline together, it may sound a bit off putting. But stay with me here.

You see, when we apply a bit of discipline in our eating habits at home, we are likely to teach our children the same. I am afraid, I am going to have to use another phrase here, 'Everything in moderation, including moderation itself'. We need to teach our children moderation in eating habits. Let's start with mealtimes. Do you enforce proper mealtimes for your children, or do you just leave them to graze and go, open and raid the fridge as frequently as they please?

Let us consider some points that may help:

- Set three proper mealtimes per day, breakfast, lunch and dinner. For in between nibbles, try and keep choices of wholesome snacks such as fruit, yoghurt, cheese and breadsticks, etc handy. Avoid encouraging younger children to find their own snacks. I can guarantee they would go for the unhealthy ones!

- Always encourage children to sit down for a meal. It's good for digestion and encourages children to eat at a good pace with the rest of the family. I admit I struggle to sit and eat my breakfast at leisure if I am in the middle of a morning rush. Yet, I have to remind myself that if I'm not disciplined, it is likely my children will probably follow my example.
- Never encourage your child to run around during mealtimes with you chasing them around the house with food and cups of milk. Research has shown that children that learn to sit down for a meal from a younger age and learn to distinguish mealtimes from playtimes, tend to be less fussy eaters and have fewer eating disorders than children who are encouraged to eat and play as they go along.
- Enforce good hand hygiene. Let your children watch you wash your hands regularly especially after using the toilet and before meals. See to it that the younger ones wash their hands with soap and water before they sit to eat.
- Make food interesting. For toddlers, make their plates appealing with colour and texture, like carrot sticks or cucumber fingers with their favourite pasta or a sandwich. Our son's favourite food in his childhood was rice with vegetables,

dal, and a drop of ghee. Could anything be more satisfying? For older children, get them to help you prepare food from start to finish. When they are familiar with the kitchen and with ingredients, their interest in food will deepen. Quite naturally, they will be more inclined to try out new dishes without fuss.

- Avoid food negotiations. Try not to swap disliked foods with their favourite ones. As a rule of thumb, I avoided trading foods with my kids if they did not like something on their plate. I made allowances for spicy food or if they were unwell or not their normal self. Otherwise, I tried to get them used to eating whatever was cooked for the family. We encouraged our kids to try everything. Now, I don't have to feel too worried about my kids fussing with food when we're invited out to dinner.
- Try not to force feed. I know the term force feeding is usually related to baby feeding. But what I mean in this context is that we have a built-in radar that can usually flag up when we feel our kids aren't eating enough. Sometimes this radar works overtime and our answer to every problem presented is, '*kuchkhaa lo*!' or '*aur khao na*!' (eat something or eat some more). However, we often forget that children's tummies are quite small and they need to develop a healthy relationship with their food before they learn to enjoy it. This

may sound like a paradox but instead of serving them larger portions to encourage them to eat, serve them smaller portions. If they finish that satisfactorily and want more, then give them a bit more. The problem starts when we, as well-meaning mothers, overload their plates and they automatically think of it as force feeding. Just the sight of the overloaded plate can make the food unappetising for our young ones. Adjust your 'radar' to what is suitable for your child.

Exercise

I think I better keep this section brief as I sadly do not have much experience-based advice to offer on this topic. Nevertheless, I will emphasise a couple of things, whether you're a gym lover or a street jogger or a 'can't-be-bothered-to-exercise-er', your attitude to physical fitness will likely rub off on your child. I know because I have seen it in my own family and kids.

Although I pushed for my children to start taking swimming lessons, I will credit my husband with helping them become competent swimmers. In fact, both my kids swim far better than I can. I am not counting on drowning anytime soon but learning to swim is a life skill I regret not being able to learn. Yet, it is still one of the items in my to-do list. It is also a great form of exercise and stress relief and the relaxing effects that swimming has on my husband and children are visible immediately.

Growing up, we played cricket and badminton every day after school. I quickly developed a love for them and became quite good at them. I now encourage my children to play sports of their choice. I find that the physical and mental benefits derived from playing sports are almost instant. Of course, everyone is different in their preference. You may laugh at me, but for me personally, I would rather spend my time doing a physical activity, which brings short term joy as well as fulfils a long term purpose.

For instance, I would much rather go for a long walk in the park with my kids and my dog than jogging aimlessly indoors on a treadmill. This way, my whole family gets some fresh air and exercise away from screens. Or I would rather expend my energy riding bikes or playing badminton with my kids than do press-ups and push-ups!

My husband would disagree with me as he would prefer putting a set time aside to work out in a gym. The point is to help children develop a love for physical activity from childhood onwards. We are living in times where half the population of the world is starved, and the other half is obese. Our choice of food and our physical activities (or lack of) are largely to blame in developed countries. It works best when we recognise this early on.

The bottom line I would advocate is, whatever diet you choose to feed your family and whatever form of regular exercise you decide to do, try to make it wholesome, enjoyable and fun for you and your family.

Chapter 21

Don't stress yourself and don't stress your children

At school

We want our children to succeed at school. We provide tuition for them and other forms of support to them to help achieve excellent grades. What's wrong with that, you might ask? Nothing, of course.

However, since starting this book, we have been feeling the effects of a global pandemic. All our lives have been changed in some form or another. We've been working from home and our children have been studying from home. Let's not mistake this as the so-called 'new normal'.

There's nothing normal about trying to survive in the middle of a battlefield. Despite enduring the effects of this pandemic we don't want our children to miss out on their education.

Many parents I have come across are seriously concerned about the effects of the pandemic on the education of their children. Their children are not just getting home-schooled, but the parents are now spending a small fortune every month subscribing to online education and catch-up courses for their four and five year olds in addition to their normal school work. They are worried that their children are falling behind in their education. Now parents therefore have resorted to keeping kids glued for hours on YouTube and other digital platforms to keep up with their academic learning as well as on line recreation. While I am just as concerned for my kids too, I can't help but think, are we taking this a bit too far? If the education of our children has been stalled by a stumbling block in the form of a pandemic, could we use this time to make a positive change? How? You know what they say, 'When life gives you lemons, make lemonade'. If you have been home schooling or plan to get them to study at home in the future, consider these pointers.

- Set age-appropriate schoolwork for your children each day. However, do not get disheartened if they are unable to finish their allocated tasks for that day. At this point, their health – mental or emotional – needs far more attention than their academic studies.
- For younger children, try to help them learn with hands on activities. For example, instead of teaching them to memorise their alphabet or their multiplication table, try to make it into a

game using songs or using play dough, paint or even pieces of pasta!

- Keep to fixed study times and keep study sessions short, especially for younger children. They have short attention spans and will be more productive when working for brief durations.
- Keep a snack and drink handy. Don't forget, our children can also get 'hangry'. As a result, they may play up during their schoolwork. Bonus tip: Take a coffee break yourself.
- Encourage them to read a variety of subjects. Start with topics that interest *them* at a young age whether they are story books, Disney books or even comics. Once they get the reading bug, you will soon find that they will devour books on other subjects too!
- If all your efforts fail, do not fret. Avoid blaming yourself or your child. For children in the primary school age group, literacy and numeracy are a couple of key skills. They can always learn about quantum physics when they are older!
- The bottom line is, whether your child is going to school or studying at home, try not to force them or put undue pressure on them. Help them to enjoy life and make each day count. Not only do they live their childhood just once but you will also only experience their childhood once. Try to make the most of it. They will appreciate it and thank you in the long run.

At home

Whether it is during normal times or during times of unprecedented circumstances, like the pandemic, things can be even more stressful and challenging. Whatever the case, we want our homes to be havens of mental peace, emotional security and unrelenting stability for ourselves as well as our children. You could be working from home, children could be studying from home, you may possibly no longer have the luxury of a domestic worker, which you so heavily relied upon before. You may have also been affected even more seriously by the pandemic than most people, for example, because of illness, bereavement or economic losses.

Any of these effects could cause even more distress and uncertainty within the family. If you're already in smaller living quarters, the lack of personal space may have been severely amplified by the pandemic. Earlier perhaps, we used to look forward to coming home to peace and quiet – our sanctuary; we now dread being back within walls. What was once our haven of solitude, became our prison.

Perhaps this was the case with you: Were you often at the end of your tether with your spouse or other relatives? Did you sometimes hide in the toilet just to get 5 minutes of quiet time away from screaming toddlers or fighting siblings? Did you regularly find yourself, like me, having to cook and clean all day long without respite to cater to various demands and menu orders? Did you feel 'zoom-ed out' after hours and hours of video conferencing either for work or school? Did you have to resort to using alcohol or taking sleep medication to help you doze off when you couldn't fall asleep naturally?

It's ok to agree with some or even all of these questions.

What is now dawning on experts is, that, we are facing the new epidemic of mental health. And we all must learn to accept one truth: It is ok to not be ok. I am not a medical professional, so I'm not aiming to prescribe or recommend any specific medicine or other forms of treatment to help combat these feelings of anxiety or clinical depression. What I can do is empathise with the situation, as I know and have worked with many people, young and old alike whose mental health struggles have become worse during the pandemic. Here are just some of my tried and tested tips to help you stay sane as part of a working family.

- Ask for help. It's simple. These three simple words mean often much more than we give them credit for. They can be the difference between feeling sad or happy, alone or sociable, angry or relaxed and in some extreme cases, life or death. You can ask for help from trusted family members, neighbours or even your doctor. Some countries also provide emergency numbers for severe cases of depression.
- Don't brush over the topic. If you are feeling down or are struggling with anxious thoughts, do not sweep them under the rug. They need to be discussed. Often times, just talking to a friend

about something that has been getting you down can be enough to put things in perspective. Once you have opened up about the subject and talked it over, you will often feel lighter and less stressed and even if you haven't *solved* the problem, you will find it's actually easier to *manage* it.

- Express yourself. In addition to verbal expression, it is often very helpful to express yourself non-verbally. How? You can take up old or new hobbies. These interests can now become a channel for you to express yourself non-verbally. Activities such as music, drawing, painting and even knitting can have a surprisingly calming and reflective effect on us. The results are often immediate.
- Avoid unhealthy forms of 'escapism'. While some people thought the pandemic to be an excellent opportunity to spend time at home, experts are now finding that alcohol consumption and overuse of prescription medication for relaxation has gone up significantly among the population. Many people have used these methods as crutches to literally 'drown their sorrows' and 'numb the pain'. Is it really wise to resort to these methods? It also affects your family and children. Don't forget, their mental health is on the line as well. In an attempt to numb our own anxiety, let us not put our mental or physical health or our children at risk.

- Do some physical activity every day. Even going for a short 20 minute walk every day can help things along. The fresh air, the exercise, the increase in blood circulation and the change of scenery can help cheer you up and you will be back home much more revitalised.
- Finally, don't worry about things that are out of your control. Lost your job during the pandemic? Or worse, lost a loved one or perhaps suffering from ill health yourself? Struggling with kids and don't know how to cope? Just take one day at a time. I once read somewhere, 'If you *can* fix a problem, then why worry? If you *can't* fix a problem, then why worry?' Both are so true in so many cases.

Bottom line is, try to keep a positive outlook. Avoid worrying unnecessarily and remember brighter days are always ahead.

Case Scenario 1

Fussy eating and overactive toddler.

One set of my parents came to me with a concern which is faced by most parents—fussy eating and hyperactivity. I went in to observe the child's typical day:

Mealtimes:

Breakfast for the child included a glass of milk with sugar and white bread with chocolate paste.

Lunch for the family consisted of a vegetable dish with rice and lentils, which the child didn't want, so was offered several other alternatives. Finally, he decided he wanted chocolate spread with bread as he refused most other options.

Snacks were mostly fried and fatty options such as chips, fried chicken, and fried cheesy snacks.

Dinner time consisted of whole wheat chapatis with sugar and butter on them accompanied by another glass of milk with sugar. He was being coaxed into eating every mouthful of all his sugar chapatis. So obviously all that sugar rush made him even more hyperactive. His pent-up energy naturally needed burning and the only way that would happen was by jumping on the sofa or tumbling all over the bed covers and cushions.

I provided the bewildered parents the following tips:

- In the mornings, encourage the child to wake up naturally using gentle morning sounds and natural sunlight where possible. This can be achieved by simply drawing the curtains open.
- Once washed and toileted, offer breakfast such

as low sugar cereals with milk and fruit or toast with butter/scrambled egg. Avoid sugary jams/ spreads as these give a short but sharp sugar rush followed by a sugar crash.

- Play time can only be allowed when mealtimes are complete. Note: this *does not* mean that the child must finish everything on his plate. Bear in mind his stomach is still small. You can proactively encourage him to finish everything on his plate by giving smaller portions in the first place.
- Ensure the child is seated for his snacks/meals. I always advise against eating while playing or chasing the child to eat mouthfuls of his food. *Meal/snack times should be kept separate from other activities.* This transition will take time however, consistency is key.
- Meals and snacks should have intervals of at least 2 hours (as this is how long it takes for a young child to build his appetite for the next food intake) failing this, a young toddler of 3 years will likely not feel hungry enough to eat properly at his next meal time.
- Make food interesting by adding texture and colour, such as crispy bread sticks with soft cheese, etc. You could even make smiley food emojis such as a pancake face with sliced grapes for eyes and an apple slice for mouth.
- Avoid swapping wholesome and nutritious meals by several alternative options. If the child isn't

eating his meals, do not threaten or plead with him to eat. Even if he does not eat his meal in its entirety in one sitting, bear in mind he will have his snacks within a couple of hours.

- Offer snacks such as sips of water/milk in a Sippy cup, chopped or sliced carrot or cucumber, or crackers and cheese cubes.

Case Scenario 2

Letting your child be unsupervised online

During one of our consultations about online safety, a parent raised a point that she trusted her ten-year-old daughter to be safe online as long as she was watching YouTube videos or playing games online. She reasoned that as schools were on and off during the pandemic children were used to being online for schoolwork and play. Working from home, she could not practically keep an eye on her daughter 24/7.

She had a point. It is never easy trying to work from home as well as manage home schooling. We discussed some benefits as well as dangers of allowing children unsupervised access to the internet:

Besides others mentioned earlier in this book, here are some online dangers.

1. Cyber bullying
2. Sexual predators
3. Emotional abuse
4. Psychological abuse
5. Pornography

6. Low self esteem
7. Identity theft
8. Fake news and misinformation
9. Extremism
10. Time mis-usage due to addiction

...to name a few...

We discussed ways in which our children may be drawn out by or exposed to such dangers through innocent looking videos and even cartoons. Although we trust them, they are still naïve and inexperienced, hence, they run the risk of putting themselves in danger as outlined above. Although we may never be able to monitor them 24/7, if we have frequent, even daily conversations with them about their online activities, they may feel more comfortable about approaching you, their parent, if they come across something of concern or inappropriate.

Examples of conversation starters:

1. "How did you get on with that game you were playing?.... Who won – you or your friend?" . . . "Glad you had fun!... Can you remind me how somebody can know whether it is genuinely his friend he is playing with and not a stranger?" – Allow them to answer in detail. Also commend them for their efforts to be alert and vigilant while online.
2. "Those craft and slime videos on YouTube are such fun, aren't they? I enjoy watching them with you also... Which one do you love the most?" – "Can you show me how to get rid of a video that

may pop up that makes you a bit uncomfortable?" – Allow them to respond in as much detail as possible, listen carefully and commend them for opening up.

3. "It's so nice you can keep in touch with your friends on your WhatsApp groups; you must miss spending time with them. Is there any particular friend you love chatting with? How do they react if someone in the group doesn't get along with another person?" – Allow them to respond without any prompts. Ensure they can feel you are genuinely interested in what they have to say.

Case Scenario 3

Tips for home-schooling during the pandemic

A parent phoned me in utter frustration about having to work from home while home-schooling. Needless to say, she was at the end of her tether with trying to juggle working full time with home-schooling three different children. She was desperately in need of assistance.

After listening to her and reassuring her that she is doing her best, I suggested that she talk me through her routine for a typical day.

She explained at length and to be fair, she *was* doing her best to give her best shot. Her husband, who was also working from home did his best to help around with chores. However, they were still struggling to cope mentally.

I suggested that Mum and Dad speak to their

respective employers to temporarily change their work timings/shifts so that Mum and Dad work opposite shifts so that while one parent needs to work undisturbed, the other parent can assume childcare duties, home-schooling etc.

If that was not possible at all or at least not possible in part, I also suggested the following tips.

1. Keep timings for lessons the same as school would have been. This would help with maintaining a routine to some extent.
2. Take frequent breaks with the children. Even if it means a 5-minute break every hour, try walking around the house, putting the laundry on, making a trip to the loo or even outside for some fresh air.
3. Keep snacks and drinks handy (but only give them out during their break times so that they have something to look forward to!).
4. If all fails, remember the bottom line that all they *really* need to learn at this stage is to read, write and count.

Case Scenario 4

Help! I am a lockdown Mummy. My baby may be lacking in early learning skills!

A few new mothers had consulted with me during the 2020 pandemic lockdown concerned that their babies were behind in their normal and expected stage of growth.

They were concerned that the babies had been born

without meeting their Dads in the delivery rooms, nor had they seen extended family and grandparents. They hadn't been outdoors much and when they did go out, they saw their parents and others masked up and armed with sanitisers, gloves, visors and other PPE.

I understood their concerns for, even though they are underrated, they happen to be topical. Babies learn from people's faces and expressions. Our lockdown babies have missed out on so much of that interaction which includes meeting and bonding with grandparents etc. There is much concern that in prolonged lockdowns, many babies may miss catching up on these major social and emotional building blocks during their early months and years of life.

My proactive tips for concerned parents include the following.

1. Encourage babies and toddlers to interact with relatives via face-to-face contact even if it is through zoom or other online options.
2. Expose babies and toddlers to verbal interaction, such as talking to them, reading to them, laughing with them and singing with them as much as possible.
3. Avoid getting tempted to 'baby-talk' with them as they will learn to form the same words and expressions that they hear from you.
4. Expose your toddler to loads of picture books with faces of people from different cultures, ages, skin colour etc.

5. Try to go out with the baby/toddler at least once a day even if it is just for a walk around the corner. This is therapeutic and healthy for you the parent as well as the baby.

Case Scenario 5

What if my child lies?

Here is another scenario I often come across when talking to parents and families. Every parent that I can think of has experienced this situation at least once in their parenting journey.

One of my parents gave me this scenario. They walked in after a long day at work and found a ball thrown across the room with a broken vase on the floor, cushions scattered everywhere and muddy shoes on the rug. She immediately understood what had happened – her child has been a bit over ambitious while at home and decided to turn the living room into a football field.

Her child was standing there with a guilty look on his face. She asked him what happened? She was exhausted, frustrated and angry... rightly so... since she had explicitly forbidden her child to play ball inside the house. She knew what had happened... as plain as day... however, her child was adamant they didn't kick the ball in the house.

Now what? She didn't want her child to get away with what he had done by lying about it. Neither did she want to punish him without him understanding what he had done.

I commended her for first stepping back and taking

stock of the situation instead of reacting rashly.

I explained to her that children tend to lie because of various reasons. They might lie to get what they want, to avoid trouble or get out of things.

Young children may lie to get your reaction or attention. Depressed or anxious kids might lie because they don't want others to worry. There are many layers involved when you discover your child has lied.

In the above scenario, the child in question was simply afraid of the reaction especially since he knew the clear cut instructions from his Mum about playing ball indoors.

I suggested the parent to do the following:

- Encourage your child to always tell the truth by setting an example yourself. For instance, avoid trying to wriggle out of a tight corner by telling a lie or making an unjustifiable excuse. Your child is watching and learning!
- Very young children often learn communication through 'cause and effect'. If they feel that admitting their mistake causes a bad reaction from their grownups, this will prevent them from admitting their fault the next time.
- Reassure your child that they'll be safe if they tell the truth.

Case Scenario 6

Managing a toddler tantrum in public

As outlined earlier in the book, many parents find it

challenging to take their child on outings especially when the child is prone to temper tantrums.

One such parent approached me with her predicament. She was terrified to take her three year old to the shops, to the park, to the cinema and even at times to the nursery.

I understood her difficulties as it can often be quite overwhelming if you are faced with an angry that is, out of control, toddler at home, let alone in public.

Advice:

Don't let the fear of a tantrum put you off taking your toddler out and about. You can be prepared as mentioned earlier.

- Preparation is key when dealing with a potential tantrum. For example, if you're taking your child to the park and worry about a tantrum, speak to your child about it in advance.
- Recognise that tantrums are a way for your child to express their 'big' feelings. These 'big' feelings can be anger, tiredness, hunger, etc and the only way they know they can get the feelings noticed is through a tantrum.
- Avoid getting angry yourself and losing your own cool, as doing so may fuel the tantrum even more.
- Remember that toddlers between the ages of 2–3 years can understand simple instructions and generally respond well to 'Yes' and 'No'.
- If the tantrum has already started and the immediate distraction technique doesn't seem

to work, be empathetic to them. Kneel down to their level, give them a hug while giving them a chance to calm themselves down.

- Don't feel embarrassed or judged if people are watching. Chances are they would have experienced something similar with their children at some point. Every child goes through a similar phrase at some point or another.
- Be confident. Even if you are terrified and bursting with nervousness yourself, try and keep yourself calm. If need be, get to your child's level. You can do some deep breathing exercise together.
- Reassure your child that you understand that they are upset and that the feeling will pass.

Case Scenario 7

How to bring up a confident child

In this day and age of self-consciousness, many children are left feeling inadequate. It boils down to how they feel they are perceived in society. Even young children can start feeling nervous enough to lose their confidence. One of my clients expressed their concerns for their child. They felt that their child was not confident or upbeat about anything. Whether it was schoolwork, hobbies, interests, talents or even speaking in front of people, the child just could not get themselves to feel confident enough to take initiatives or complete their work.

In cases such as this, it is always recommended from the outset, that parents observe their child closely in different situations before they decide their child isn't confident with their tasks or assignments. Are they overly conscious of themselves? Do they feel that expectations are too high? Are they experiencing any other serious challenges within or outside the family home such as bullying, exploitation etc?

Once parents had an idea of where the problem may be stemming from, I suggested they could take the following steps.

- Regularly spend one-to-one time with their child doing relaxed activities that interest their child, such as painting, drawing, reading etc.
- Gently let your child take the lead in those activities they choose to do with your full support along the way. Such as, if the child wants to paint with you but you would rather do a less messy activity, avoid enforcing your own plans.
- Regularly offer *genuine* praise, not just blanket praise such as, 'good boy/girl'. Be specific such as, 'I love the way you choose colours' or 'it is good you were so careful to spread an old cloth to save the table from any paint spots etc?
- Avoid scolding them at every given opportunity. Even if they have perhaps spilt some paint or a drink or dropped some crumbs on the floor, avoid jumping in and scolding them. Accept that accidents can happen with anyone. We may be more careful now, but surely, we also had our little accidents when we were younger!

- Avoid creating a tense atmosphere when your child is around you. They will, without any doubt, sense it. It will make them become edgy and nervous themselves.
- Listen, really listen, to their thoughts and feelings. Whether you are doing school runs, during meals or bath times, converse with them. Be sure to listen attentively to what they have to say. When they feel that you are totally with them, their sense of self-worth will gradually increase.
- Your alert and *undivided* attention is essential, even for short spans of time.

Case Scenario 8

Help! My child doesn't listen to me

This is a common parenting experience. I also have been through this myself – many of my clients have had similar experiences with this problem. Once a mother approached me with the concern that her eight year old simply wouldn't listen to her. The child has no problem listening to her Dad or grandparents and has good behaviour reports from school. But for some reason, she simply doesn't listen to her Mum.

Some typical examples were when the mother asks her eight-year-old daughter to turn the screens off, she will ignore the instructions; when Mum calls her for dinner, she won't turn up; when Mum tries to get her to do homework, the daughter will ignore her and so on.

I listened with empathy as this is a fairly common

phenomenon among children, where they tend to listen to one parent more than the other. However in this case, it was a bit more severe, as the child seemed to listen to everyone else except her mother! It appeared that the problem was either in the mother's methods or the daughter simply didn't know where she stood with her Mum. Her confusion led the young girl to decide to mentally 'mute' her mother.

My observations:

Within a couple of hours, the issue became apparent. Mum was certainly giving out instructions, however, she was glued to her phone at the same time. She would barely lift her head up from her phone and failed to command the attention of her daughter. The daughter would in turn, respond in a haphazard manner and carry on with whatever she was doing. Mum would also become quickly exasperated and resort to repeatedly nagging and shouting at the daughter. I also observed the interaction of the other family members. As soon as the Mum calls her daughter, Granny interrupts to tell the child to fetch her glasses. Mum, still busy on her phone, keeps calling the child. Dad comes in, calls the child over and tells her to do something else.

I advised the mother the following course of action:

- The first step to get your child to listen to you is to form a connection with them. Level with them by taking an interest in them and all their activities on a daily basis. Communicate with them *without* the distraction of phones, screens and other gadgets.

- Discuss with your spouse and other relatives the importance of all being on the same page. Everyone needs to take turns when speaking to the child. On this occasion, the child was being subject to various voices all at the same time. Instructions were being dished out from all without giving the child the time or occasion to complete them one by one.. The child can only focus on one task at a time, hence, she automatically only carried out the latest set of instructions fresh on her mind (which happened to be Dad's).
- Avoid giving your child instructions while you're on your phone or computer as inevitably our own attention would be divided. By doing so we are setting the wrong precedent. The child would automatically understand, 'If Mum/Dad are not focussed on what they are telling me, maybe it's not important anyway. I don't really need to pay attention either.'
- For effectiveness, call your child to you, kneel down to their level, make eye contact and get their attention *before* speaking to them. Once you've given your instruction, get them to repeat it to you so you know that they've understood what it is you want them to do.
- Ask your family members to be observant. They need to be alert to know that if your child is already busy doing something, they need to

employ the same method of getting the child's attention.

Case scenario 9

Help! I just lost my temper with my child

Surely, we have all done this at some point in our parenting journey.

One of the scenarios I am regularly presented is just this feeling of guilt, regret as well as helplessness. I can say, hand on heart, I empathise with this.

A parent approached me with this problem. He had lost his temper with his child. The parent had just finished a hard day at work and was mentally exhausted. He sat down to unwind while his toddler was so excited to see Daddy that he started bouncing on top of him demanding Dad play with him. Dad couldn't muster up the energy to play just then yet the demands of the toddler were relentless. Eventually Daddy lost his cool and shouted at the child to get off him and go to his Mum! Immediately, after his explosive outburst, the Dad felt bad and remorse seeped in. Why had he been so harsh? Why couldn't he have been more patient? Why did he lose his cool? His child was only asking for his time – why couldn't he give it to him?

I listened with some of my own flashbacks and recognised that this is a problem more common than we realise. I explained to Dad the following suggestions.

We carry so many stresses all day long – work stresses, family stresses, maybe even health worries for our family and the pandemic may have increased these pressures and added new ones. As humans ourselves, we are not created to handle intense pressures for a prolonged period of time. We are bound to let go of these pressures in some form. Often it results in us dumping our stresses on our kids. Not because we want to hurt them but because, it is an unplanned reaction to a situation. I recommended that next time Dad is faced with this situation, he could try out the following pattern proactively to contain his fatigue.

- Prepare in advance. If you've had a difficult day, give yourself a few minutes to unwind without anyone near you. Whether it is in your car or walking home or even in your office. Switch off from your work mode to relax mode – listen to soothing music or the radio or read a few chapters of a favourite book. Do this for 15 – 20 minutes *before* you get home.
- Once you're home, greet everyone at home. Do allow 5 – 10 minutes for the excitement of your child(ren) to wear off. This shouldn't last long, during which, give them lots of love, hugs and your undivided attention.
- If you still lose your cool, despite your best efforts, immediately apologise to your child. Say something like, 'I am so sorry I shouted at you. Mum/Dad is very tired and not really feeling very well at this moment. I missed you so much and was looking forward to seeing you all day. I didn't

think I would be so tired when I came home. Will you forgive me and give me 15 minutes to freshen up. After that maybe we can play that game you wanted to play? Thank you for being such a sensible boy/girl about it.'

- Finally, forgive yourself. It's human to make mistakes and once we recognise that – half the battle is won. Our acceptance with a willingness to improve on our own mistakes has a bonus! We will be willing to accept the mistakes of others too.

Case Scenario 10

How do I deal with sibling rivalry

'The best gift you can give your child is a sibling.' This may feel correct but may not often seem so from your child's perspective. Sibling rivalry is something at least two thirds of parents will have to contend with. If you had siblings growing up, you would know what I am talking about. As with me and my siblings, there were no shortage of squabbles, disagreements, and mutual irritations. Despite that we also learned other life skills like negotiation techniques, people skills, learning to share, taking turns in a group, to name a few.

Some parents have asked me to give them a few tips to help them effectively manage their children's quarrels.

My tips are the following...

- Avoid getting involved in petty squabbles. In the long run your children will benefit by learning to fight their own battles, most of the time.

- Encourage them to share but avoid forcing them to share *everything* with each other. They need to have a sense of belonging and ownership of a small number of their own toys and items.
- Let them know that it is ok to disagree with each other as long as they can disagree respectfully for example—without hurling insults, name calling or physically attacking each other.
- Let them understand that it may sometimes be ok to quarrel but to forgive is definitely more important.
- Avoid taking sides unless you absolutely must. The exception to this rule would be if you need to intervene to avoid things getting out of hand in the form, for example, of a physical fight that may result in injury or damage to any important household item.
- Always encourage them to make peace before bedtime. This is a highly recommended practice that will serve them well even when they grow older, and each have their own families.
- Recognise that it is not fair to expect that your older child will automatically gel with a new-born sibling. Bonding takes time and patience. In the meantime, do everything to avoid letting your older child feel that they're losing your attention and love by giving them one-to-one attention while baby is being looked after by Dad or other relatives.

Case Scenario 11

Dealing with negativity and interference from relatives when parenting your child

Many of my clients live in a Nuclear or Core Family, which comprises of both parents and children. There are other families also, such as, Joint, and Blended families.

One of my clients recently approached me with a specific problem which she found quite challenging. This was what she called constant negativity and interference from her extended family such as her parents as well as her in-laws. Both sets of grandparents felt that they could use their own years of parenting experiences of raising their own children to help the younger parents.

Some of the parents' concerns were that the grandparents seemed to over ride certain ground rules that Mum was trying to set such as her child's bedtime routines and eating habits. On top of that she also felt judged and criticised by the grandparents with certain comments such as, 'You don't discipline enough, the child is getting spoiled', 'You aren't feeding him well, he is skinny', 'You aren't building up her immunity, she's always getting sick', etc. This was no doubt affecting the mother's own self confidence but also her relationship with her husband, besides confusing the children as well.

Here is my advice to her.

- Let your husband get on board with the situation, by having a heart-to-heart conversation. Avoid being critical about his parents as he may feel defensive. Just share your concerns as to what effect their comments are beginning to have on your mental health and confidence level.

- Come to a mutual agreement with your husband as to how you both will deal with external criticism of your parenting methods.
- Next, have a family meeting with the grandparents and respectfully address the matter. Reassure them that you value their input and support. Certainly, they are welcome to offer suggestions. However, as a parent yourself, you both need to make a final decision on setting the child's routine.
- Be specific that you understand they have the best interests of the child at heart, and you are grateful for their suggestions. However, as grandparents, they have a cherished role in keeping peace and respect within the family including maintaining respect of the child's parents. If they feel that improvements could be made, they must feel free to speak with you and your spouse outside the earshot of the child. Reassure them that you value their blessing and involvement in your child's life.

Case Scenario 12

Helping your teenager to use phones responsibly

Teenage years are often some of the most interesting years in a child/adolescent's life. Why so? Your child is graduating from being a child to an 'adult-in-training'.

Some of my clients find that the teenage years go by

with smooth-sailing, while there are others who don't think so.

One such example is of a parent who came to me with the following problem. Her teenage son was always too preoccupied with being on his phone.

He wasn't allowed to be on his phone at school. However, at other times, he just could not manage staying away from his phone. It wasn't that he was viewing inappropriate online material. He was genuinely just busy texting his friends or playing online games or spending time on educational chat forums. The parents' main concern was the amount of time that he was on his phone.

I understood the concern as we are living in the digital age where everything is accessible on a phone in the palm of your hand, from education to games, from music to directions. The more serious concern is that such behaviour can become highly addictive. .

I suggested the following possible ways to deal with this issue.

- Have a frank and open discussion about screen usage (including phones) within the family. Share your concerns with your teenager. Ask him/her what apps and programs they enjoy the most on their phones and ask them to come up with suggestions to reduce phone usage. Come to a mutual agreement—and stick to it !
- Lead by example—there is no point trying to drive through a change in phone habits in your children if they regularly view us, the grownups,

glued to our phones.

- Have a few screen-free evenings with the family. Spend time playing good old fashioned board games, cooking meals together or even reading together.
- Set a ground rule of not allowing phones to interrupt family meals – including your own phones.
- If things start to slide, try using certain apps which monitor your teenager's phone usage. Make sure that you discuss the details with your teenager – the specific benefits of using these apps. If they feel that this intrudes on 'their privacy' you know the problem is deeper than you realise, in which case, you may need to try and review your teenager's phone privileges.

Case Scenario 13

How do I genuinely praise my child?

Praising your child isn't often difficult as you will agree we all will find plenty of things to praise our children for.

The trouble comes, however, when we cannot differentiate between genuine praise and empty praise. One such problem was presented to me by a parent and his concern was the following: Growing up, this Dad's upbringing was not trouble free. He rarely received praise from his father and any efforts he made at school or sports' or any other extra-curricular activities, never met his father's expectations. This reaction often left him feeling downcast and dejected. This also led to feelings of resentment and stubbornness as he grew up. Now that he is a parent himself, he doesn't want to repeat the same mistakes with his own child. Instead, he often finds himself going overboard with too much praise for things that his child doesn't see as a challenge.

I suggested the parent think of the following points.

- Genuinely praising a child is crucial for their self-esteem, confidence, and mental health. It also helps them to develop a proper view of themselves and their abilities.
- It's a myth to say that 'praising a child too much never hurt him'. It *can* be harmful for him in the long run. For example – your child hates maths. Yet you praise them to the skies for completing just half of their homework. All the while you do know that they aren't inclined to even *try* to complete the rest of their homework up to standard. Would they understand the value of putting in extra effort or going out of their comfort zone to learn something they don't enjoy?
- Avoid blanket praise. This serves no purpose. Suppose you overhear your child being polite or kind to someone, instead of just saying, 'good boy/girl' specify the reason for the praise, 'I am so pleased to hear you remembered to say thank you' or 'I love how kind you were to friend by sharing your toys with them'.

- Use praise as a reward instead of a bribe *after* they complete their task. When they hate brushing their teeth, tell them how lovely and shiny their teeth look *after* they've been brushed properly. This will help them to understand that in order to gain their reward they need to make some effort. This will lead them to *value* the praise and take pride in their efforts.

Case Scenario 14

How do I deal with Mom guilt?

Mom guilt is so common these days. Although we have all kinds of machines and gadgets to simplify our lives, somehow our modern lives have become even more busy and complicated than we expected. Add to these pressures from social media and other external influencers.

One such problem was presented to me by a Mum who was struggling with her mental health. She needed to go out to work to help support the family. Yet while juggling childcare and housework etc – she was at the end of her tether. She also had low self-esteem largely contributed by her social media feed which contained pictures of seemingly perfect lives of other Mums and influencers. A cocktail of these issues was really bringing her down as well as affecting her confidence as a parent.

I listened to the parent's concerns with empathy as understandably we all face similar challenges where we feel we have to be a perfect super Mum on heels who is able to effortlessly and competently tackle everything that life throws at her, and she of course, never has a bad day!

I suggested to her the following tips:

- Every day when you wake up, take a deep breath and count 3 things that you are thankful for each day.
- Get into the habit of taking a 15 minute 'me' time twice a day without any screens. Include things such as reading a book with a cup of coffee, taking a warm and comforting bath, listening to music, window shopping, buying yourself a bunch of flowers etc.
- For a period of time, take a break from social media and any one in your friend circle that brings you negativity or makes you feel worse about yourself.
- It is commendable that you want to give of yourself to your family, but you must regularly fill your own basket with your emotional needs before you can give of your best self to others.
- Find a friend to talk to – someone who is a mature, older, and more experienced mother perhaps. They may be of a different generation, but it may surprise you to have their ear and receive their pearls of wisdom.

Case Scenario 15

What is Toxic Parenting?

Toxic Parenting is often talked about these days. During

recent years, a few parents have approached me about their realisation of having been victims of toxic parenting from their own parents while growing up. This has caused them to be conscious of their own parenting methods towards their children. Part of my response to them was to listen to their concerns and feelings and look at situations from their points of view.

With a couple of parents, I have had to help them differentiate between memories of a tough childhood with memories of a toxic childhood.

Typical examples of tough childhood can be (although not exclusively) the following experiences.

- Hard working parents with little means of living. They work hard to provide the basics for their children such as food, clothing, good education etc.
- Treats are a rarity, if at all. You often have to wear hand-me-down clothes etc.
- You may come from a single parent family and/or be raised by extended relatives.
- You may have struggled at school with bullying or inadequate support.
- You may have had a childhood illness or lived with family that may have a member with a sustained long term illness, which may have impacted your happiness.
- You may have experienced a bereavement or a loss in the family.

While the above situations may have made your childhood trying and difficult, your general mental and emotional well being may not have been impacted in the long run.

In contrast to the above, I mentioned to these parents some typical examples of toxic parenting:

- The parent may be overly self-centred and consumed by their own feelings and opinions.
- They may down play your feelings or repeatedly make you feel as if 'it's all in your head'.
- They may seek to control aspects of your life even when you are older.
- They are harsh and critical of your every effort or achievement.
- They may make you feel inadequate and insufficient.
- They may repeatedly make you their 'emotional punching bag'.

These are just a few examples of toxic parenting methods that are often seen to impact childhood development.

Case Scenario 16

How do I get my child to trust me?

Surely you will agree that any caring and responsible parent would want to build a good measure of trust with their child. To have a trusting relationship with someone, you require consistency, continuous work and it is a lifelong process.

Whenever any parents approach me for advice on building trust between them and their child, I first try to work with them to establish if there are any barriers that they find to building this trust? I discuss with them questions such as – Why do they feel their child may lack trust in them? What can they do in their own opinion to build a trusting relationship with their child? How committed are they to follow through with work required to build on the relationship? How willing are they to work towards recognising and protecting their children from dangers that lie ahead for them?

As I believe that nothing is worse than betraying a child's trust, I always make sure that my parents are on board 100%. Once I am convinced of their genuine commitments, I suggest to them the following possible paths.

- Be open and honest with your child. For instance, if you are going out, avoid telling them the opposite or hiding from them and leaving. Mean what you say!
- Avoid telling them make believe stories that fairies and monsters will reward or punish them for their actions – as doing so may reduce the desired effect of discipline to them. Also if the so-called 'fairy or monster' doesn't reward or punish them, your words will not matter for long.

Case Scenario 17

How can I motivate my child to study?

Children and learning go hand in hand. As you may

have read previously, I believe in encouraging very young children to learn through play. As they grow older, however, their learning gets more streamlined and organised especially when they start school.

During the pandemic, however, most schools around the world were closed. Children were at home to be home schooled by parents, many of whom were already working from home.

So, when some parents approached me with this particular situation, I suggested to them some practical tips which tend to work when applied well.

- *Make a timetable:* If you are home schooling your child, try and maintain some structure such as school timings and lessons.
- *Take frequent breaks:* Study can become a tiring chore. Without a break, your child will lose interest. Hence, take frequent and timed breaks to keep them refreshed and motivated.
- *Keep snacks and drinks handy*: The last thing you want your child to become while studying is 'hangry' – hungry and angry. Also, if you keep the meals and snacks properly timed instead of letting them graze all day long, this will help them separate study time with break time. Make sure they are well hydrated and avoid fizzy drinks while they study.
- *Encourage reading and maths*: If despite your best efforts you struggle to keep them focussed, encourage them to read and practice maths in the

form of mathematical games etc.

- *Try to make studying fun:* Depending on the age and ability of your child get them to research certain topics that they may be learning about in school. Make educational visits such as museums, zoos, libraries, ancient monuments etc., and get them to connect their existing knowledge to new things. Make these topics come to life for them.
- *Know what is going on:* Most importantly, take an interest in what they are learning in school. There is no point in insisting that they do their revision or study every day if they don't feel that you are interested in what they are learning.

Case Scenario 18

How do I deal with an angry child?

I have come across my fair share of angry children. Enough to know, that dealing with an angry toddler may not be a piece of cake.

One such situation was presented to me by a concerned parent. She was concerned that overnight her child had become angrier and more aggressive. He would refuse to get ready for school. He started habitually refusing to eat, knowing how it upset his Mum. He also started hitting and kicking his parents whenever they tried to talk to him or get him ready for school etc.

I had worked with this child before. I knew that this new behaviour was not the result of an underlying issue such as learning difficulty or special educational needs.

The child was also perfectly normally behaved at school and other settings. It was just toward his parents that he felt he could direct his anger. I first had to establish if there had been any changes or developments within the family or surroundings such as a new child or bereavement etc. Once I understood the family circumstances, I suggested the following actions to his parents:

- Every day spend some one-to-one time with the child doing an activity that the child enjoys. It can be playing with lego, colouring, playing in the park or even a video game. Key is for each parent to spend this one-to-one time with their child without any interruption. I suggested that this should be done twice a day for 15 minutes with each parent.
- Avoid waiting for an angry moment or tantrum to erupt before spending time with the child, as your child will misunderstand that the one-to-one time is a reward for being angry with his parents. Choose a time when you both are relaxed and the child is happy. For instance, the moment when one is sitting by their bed and stroking their hair before the start of the day. The idea is to build a connection with the child *before* you have to deal with the anger.
- Pick your battles – as a parent we can't always control everything and must often choose what situations we can tackle head on. Sometimes it's best to give in before giving out. For example if

your child demands an ice cream before dinner and you are about to tell them that they must wait until after dinner, however your spouse gives in to the child, it might be best to let go of that issue rather than have a face-off with your child as well as your spouse and become the bad guy.

Case Scenario 19

How do I discipline my child without threats?

At some point in your parenting journey, you are bound to come across situations where you have to administer discipline. As discussed in the earlier part of the book, discipline can be characterised either positively or negatively. While many parents these days are actively learning and looking for ways to administer positive discipline, often other parents choose to employ the method of parenting that they were brought up in, which included disciplining the child using threats.

A parent recently brought this situation to my attention. He had been brought up in the old conservative view that 'children should be seen, not heard'. He had vivid memories of his own parents employing negative discipline such as threats of punishment, sending him and his siblings to bed without dinner, taking away privileges such as play time, toys, even smacking and hitting the children.

This gentleman, now a parent himself, didn't want to use the same age-old methods on his own children and wanted to use other more positive processes.

I commended him for reaching out and trying to learn about more effective methods of parenting than those used by his parents.

I gave him the following pointers.

- Threats of punishment are not the same as giving warnings for misbehaviour. Warnings are a good tool for administering positive discipline. They drive home the idea about 'cause and effect' where the child must understand that they inevitably face consequences for their actions – good or bad.
- Giving empty threats are probably the worst because not only do they lose the effectiveness of the discipline, but they give the child the impression that your words do not matter.
- Instead of having to rely on dealing with an offence afterwards, be assertive about your child's behaviour. Give them instructions and lay out consequences for following or not following those instructions beforehand. For example, you've asked your child to go and get ready to go to bed and your child ignores your repeated requests. You finally lose your cool, shout at them and threaten to take away their screen time the next day. The next day arrives and you've forgotten your threats and the child continues as if nothing has happened. This inconsistency in delivering a warning and but not following through can be quite damaging to your child in the long run.
- Threats are often made in the heat of the moment.

A better idea would be to pre-empt the situation and offer one initial warning and a final warning along with consequences.

- I suggested to the parent to follow my workshops on administering positive discipline.

Case Scenario 20

Parents too can say, 'Sorry'

Saying 'sorry' often doesn't come naturally to us adults. The lesser we are willing to apologise the lesser our children would spontaneously feel the need to admit an error or poor behaviour. The key is not the word 'sorry', it is the realisation of having done something wrong or hurt someone. One parent asked me if she is correct to force her child to say 'sorry' for misbehaviour either at home or with peers.

Whilst I agreed that teaching our children to apologise for an offence or misbehaviour is certainly part of responsible parenting. However, I advised her that instead of forcing a child to *say* 'sorry' it is more important that they *feel* 'sorry'. How can that be achieved?

One example would be if the child has snatched a toy from another child. Everyone is watching and you find out and are understandably upset. You grab your child by hand take them to the other child, take the toy from your child and give it back to the offended child. You then sternly look at your child and command, 'say 'sorry'!'. Your child grumpily and reluctantly repeats, 'sorry'.

What lesson have we taught our child on this

occasion? The child has basically learned that as long as they commit an offence, get caught, say they're sorry they are safe and sound! No harm, no foul!

Instead, if we encourage them to *feel* sorry they are learning empathy. With this understanding, they will be less likely to repeat an offense with someone else and repeat the whole cycle again.

Ways in which you can teach them to *feel* sorry before saying it.

- If your child has committed an offence, instead of disciplining them straightaway, reach out to their level, get them to think about how they would feel if someone else hurt them or took their toy away. How would that make them feel?
- Once your child understands how it feels if the same offence happened to them, ask them directly, 'Do you feel bad that you hurt your friend'? ___ 'If you do, what should you say to your friend?'___
- Encourage your child to give up something of theirs as a gift to make peace with their friend.

Case Scenario 21

Apologising to your child is good

You will find that in your parenting journey, you will have plenty of circumstances where you may need to be the one apologising to your child. Why is it important to never miss any opportunity to apologise to your child?

One parent was surprised to hear this and she

challenged my view. This is my reasoning.

When we offend or hurt another person, someone we greatly love and respect, we immediately apologise. Why? Because we don't want our relationship with the person we have offended to go sour.

Now what about when the same person has offended us? We are naturally hurt and upset. All kinds of feelings go through our minds and hearts. We wonder—how can they treat us this way? Why did they not hear our side of the story? Why did they take away some of my privileges even though I've done nothing wrong? What did I do to deserve this? Then the offender realises their mistake and comes and apologises to me and admits that they made a mistake. They agree that they should have checked all the facts before reacting. They sincerely apologise and how does that make us feel? No doubt, relieved....

You also feel that your measure of love and respect has gone up for the person. Why? Because you recognise that they are human and make mistakes but more importantly, instead of shrugging off their mistakes, they own up to it and apologise for that. This process is a huge relationship and trust booster.

Now you can apply the same principle to the relationship between you and your child. When you apologise to your child for misjudging them or punishing them unreasonably or losing your cool with them, apologising—sincerely apologising will play a huge part in strengthening that trust between you and your child.

Examples of apologies:

- 'I am so sorry darling. I didn't realise that you had already done what I had asked. Thank you for responding to me kindly.'
- Papa may like to speak up, 'Mummy is very sad that she shouted at you. Mummy was very tired today. Will you please forgive her?'
- 'I am very sorry I was late for your play today. Mummy told me how disappointed you were. I heard how great you were...! I will do my best to attend your play next time.'

Case Scenario 22

Choosing friends for your child

As with me, did you also periodically prearrange your children's play dates for them when they were younger?

When the children are younger, they may often make their own friends without prejudice at school or nursery. Once they get older and start gravitating towards certain classmates whether it is through interests, gender or circumstances, you may find that they may organise their own friend circle.

A parent once asked me for tips on helping her child build healthy friendships. She felt her child was very shy and an introvert and would often refuse invitations to his classmates' homes for parties or sleepovers etc. Even when she organised children's parties at home, he was reluctant to help with hosting or even participating in activities.

After listening to her describe her child's personality and habits, I helped her to understand the following:

- I agreed with her that all children need social interaction with friends and similar aged peers to help them become well rounded and learn good communication and interaction skills.
- If a child is naturally shy or reserved, it doesn't automatically mean that they are introvert. They may be more of an 'observer' rather than a 'participant'. This is not always a bad thing. This means that the child is 'in' the present and his 'mind' is actively working.
- If your child doesn't care for the company of similar aged peers or his classmates in general, try involving him in groups of people with different ages, such as a mix of older people as well as younger ones. You may find that your child feels more comfortable in a mixed age group.
- If you have organised a children's party at home, ask assistance from your child about the guests *they* would like to invite. For example, make a comprehensive list of people you and your child know and ask your child to tick the ones they like to include in the event.
- Avoid forcing friendships. If your child feels uncomfortable around certain people, be observant of and considerate about this.
- Caution! Avoid accepting invitations to every children's party and sleepover, especially when

you have little or no information about who will be in-charge and who will be attending. I don't wish to alarm you but some parents can be oblivious and naïve to potential dangers to their child's safety. It's always better to be safe than sorry!

Bottom line: While it is crucial that children learn social skills through friends, you may find that good friendships do not have to be limited to the same age group.

Case Scenario 23

Being a role model for your child

I am sure you will agree that we all want to be good role models for our children. This is a question I ask many times. One recent scenario was when a new Dad asked me about the steps, he could take to be a good role model. He himself grew up in a single parent family *without* his Dad. He was the oldest of his siblings and had grown up with his Mum working full time. So he had to step up to be ready to try and help his mother around the house and with his siblings.

I commended him for wanting and trying to learn to be a good Dad. I also reassured both parents that as new parents, they both will no doubt feel a bit overwhelmed sometimes by this new responsibility and joy in their lives. While this is normal and to be expected, it need not be an impossible task and they can make a success of it.

My suggestions to them include the following tips.

- As advised in this book before, be a 'present Dad' from day 1. Be involved and interested in ante-natal classes and appointments with your spouse. Read up on all maternity related matters, whether they are hormonal changes or other medical, emotional or even financial conditions..
- Be in the delivery room for the birth. Research shows that when Dads are present for the birth, they find that bonding with their baby comes much easier.
- Be involved in the care of the baby. I don't just mean holding the baby for cuddles and kisses, but take turns with Mum for nappy changing duties, bath time and helping with bottle feeding (if you both chose to do so)
- Many Dads may consider reading to a new-born baby unnecessary. However, you will find that your baby will start picking up and responding early on to changes in tone of voice, facial expressions and even colours and patterns.
- Always try and be home for family meals as your child grows older. You will find that a steady and stable routine such as having family meals together at least once a day will set the tone for the family to become closer as the months and years go by.
- Decide early on the type of parent you wish be. Do you want to be a 'Gardener' or a 'Builder'? A Gardener is someone who knows how to nurture

and nourish his plants and soil to produce the best results. He is patient, caring and attentive. A Builder is someone who may have to be rough and tough sometimes, he knows what to build and what type of foundation he needs to put under the building. He knows what materials he needs to use to build and how to fix if something is broken.

- Be conscious of being around your children as they grow up. While you may want to give them a good life, maybe even a better one than you had growing up. However, once your children are older and reflect back upon their childhood, they may not remember the 'finer things' in life they had, but they will remember their parents' time and attention.

Case Scenario 24

My child is being bullied at school

When your child complains about being bullied at school, it can be very stressful and confusing to understand what to do.

One of the children I regularly worked with, had been complaining about being bullied at school. I raised my concerns with his parents as they needed to be aware of this also. The parents and I decided to tackle this problem first by speaking with the child about different instances of this alleged bullying and make a timeline based on the events and on what the child could remember. It was crucial for the parents and I to work together in this scenario as the child had confided in me but being the parents, they needed to be aware as well.

I suggested to the parents to deal with this in the following manner.

- Remember that bullying can take various forms such as cyber bullying, bullying at school, in the school bus, within the family home
- Note down details of the alleged bullying, such as names of the people involved, and any other children involved, the time frames based on the child's recollections. This is important to ascertain whether this bullying was a pattern or a one-off occurrence.
- Reassure your child that you believe them and that bullying of any kind is not acceptable and needs to stop.
- The child may worry about being called a 'snitch' or 'tell-tale' by his friends. Reassure him that even if that may happen, it would have taken him a lot of courage to come and report the bullying. You need to make clear you are proud of them.
- Recognise that children who bully other children may often be victims of bullying themselves. They may need help and protection as well.

Case Scenario 25

Help! I've been told my child is a bully!

As explained earlier, bullying can take various forms.

There are times when your child may experience bullying. There may also be times when on the flip side, your child may be accused of being the bully. What do you do then?

A recent case I had to deal with was when a parent was visibly upset as her child had been accused of bullying other children. She couldn't believe it and needed my help to get her to examine this situation.

I consoled her and reassured her that this phase is something many children go through at some point in their lives. Here are some pointers I gave her.

- You may feel an urge to defend or blame your child. Please avoid both without hearing the full facts. Misunderstandings can and do happen. It is essential to be fair in our dealings.
- Help your child to develop empathy for others by being kind and considerate in big things as well as little things.
- Invite your child's friends for play dates or to the parks with your child to help you observe them at play from a distance. This will give you an insight on their playing styles and hence will help you deal with any untoward behaviours that may surface.
- Avoid puffing up your child's ego by statements such as, 'You are better than everyone' or 'Show them who's the boss' etc.
- As mentioned earlier, being bullied often leads to bullying others so be open to the possibility that your child might have experienced bullying

behaviour from someone else as well.

Case scenario 26

Earning not demanding respect of my child

In my experience, many cultures hold respecting their elders in high regard. While I uphold this view also, I am of the belief that we adults should earn our respect from our children rather than demand it. How is this possible?

During one of my workshops, a parent raised this question asking what steps she could take to earn that respect from her two children.

I suggested the following tips to her.

- Build the habit to maintain trust in your child. A relationship of mutual trust promotes respect.
- Let your words matter! When you instruct your child to do something, such as washing their hands or switching their screens off, avoid nagging them. If you keep ordering them—do this, do that, do this, do that... they will eventually 'mute' you. When you 'mute' someone you don't really need to hear what they're saying. Don't let that happen between you and your child.
- Follow through with consequences. If your child doesn't do what you've asked and *you've given them a warning,* make sure you carry out the consequences you've given them. Therefore, always be realistic with the punishments you are willing to impose.
- Keep your word: Make sure to make only those

promises that you can realistically keep. Small or big ones, promises can lift your child to a new height. They can work as incentives to motivate them to do what you want them to do. However, if you fail to keep what you've promised then you are basically shattering your child's sense of trust.

Case Scenario 27

Why should I respect my child?

Earning the respect of your child is one thing, you respecting your child is another. Yet wait a minute, both actually go hand in hand!

What do I mean? In one of my workshops, we discussed trust between a parent and child as mentioned earlier. A parent asked me why respecting their child was emphasised?

I helped her to understand that in any relationship, trust is a two-way street. You wouldn't respect someone who you know doesn't respect you no matter how much they yell out from the rooftops demanding that people respect them. I gave her the following pointers.

- You can respect children even in their younger years. For example, you can respect the fact that they are unique in their abilities, interests and likes. Even younger children can have personalities that may be unique in their own way.
- Recognise that every child's level of understanding and needs are different. Even two children from

the same family can have different emotional and physical needs and your parenting methods would need to adapt to suit each child.

- Give them the dignity they deserve. For example, avoid negative discipline by embarrassing them or shaming them for their mistakes whether in public or private.
- Avoid using physical threats against them. While some parents may feel justified in smacking their children, hurting your child physically or emotionally in the name of discipline is far from giving them respect and dignity.
- Give them age-appropriate space and room to think especially if they need to mull over a misbehaviour either in word or deed. Also allow them some privacy when doing things such as toileting or changing clothes.
- Never ever betray their confidence. If they've confided something to you but you know that you must tell one other person, explain this directly to your child first. For example, if your child has confided in you that they have been a victim of bullying or abuse etc., and is terrified to disclose it to anyone else, reassure them of your trust and care for them, by saying something like, 'I know you don't want me to tell anyone, but darling, it is important that I tell somebody so that this doesn't happen to you or anyone else again. Remember that you are strong, and I

believe you. Surely, I will be with you and you will not have to face this person who hurt you if you don't want to.'

Case Scenario 28

Why do children need to learn empathy?

Empathy can be described as 'your pain in my heart.'

Not too long ago, I worked with a family who believed that boys should be raised up in an environment with strong egos and were expected to be 'macho men' when they're older.

I had training sessions and workshops with this family and helped them overcome this barrier in their parenting style. I helped them to understand that both boys and girls alike need to grow up learning to be empathetic. I discussed with them the following:

- Empathy helps promote long term and successful friendships and relationships. It also helps to prevent misunderstandings and conflicts in friendships. For example, we want people to understand if we've had a rough day, the same goes for our children, they need us to understand if they've had a difficult day.
- When we show empathy to our children in small ways and big, this rubs off on them. For example, if they are terrified of spiders, show them that you care by acknowledging their fear. Maybe you too can share with them some of your own fears. When you empathise with them, in a way, you

are levelling with them. By doing so, you will find it easier to help them overcome their fears rather than drag that fear with them into their later years.

- Empathy helps prevent feelings of jealousy, paranoia and suspicion, three qualities which can severely harm relationships.
- Empathy helps us to realise just like our children, we too were once young and inexperienced. We needed to be given a second chance. When children see us exercise empathy with them, they are likely to imitate this emotion. Empathy is a great personality asset that remains useful to the child throughout their lives.

Case Scenario 29

How can I be a patient parent?

Patience is something that is easy to wish for but incredibly hard to acquire.

One of my parents asked me how they could be a more patient parent. Make no mistake, she knew she was more patient than her spouse. However, she often found herself losing her cool with her children no matter how much she tried to remain calm and tolerant.

These were my suggestions to her:

- Make a list of things that repeatedly trigger her loss of patience. Are they related to children, her spouse, work, household chores?
- Is she able to fill her 'basket' of emotional needs

every day? Or does she allow herself to pile up all the stresses and irritation of the day?

- Avoid trying to achieve being a perfect Mum, perfect wife and a perfect professional. These don't exist. Rather, make a realistic list of your priorities and try to achieve 3 main priorities every day.
- Don't wait until you reach the end of your tether before dealing with stressful situations such as sibling squabbles. You may find that you will more likely lose your cool by waiting till it becomes too much
- Take a deep breath, get yourself a glass of water and drink very slowly. Research shows that doing this helps you to calm your nerves, reduces your blood pressure and settles your 'fight or flight' mode.
- Remove yourself from the situation. As long as nobody is in any physical danger, remove yourself from the tense situation – even if it means locking yourself in the toilet for 10 minutes until you calm down.

Case Scenario 30

What do I do if my child is physically violent?

Many times, I have had a parent ask me this question.

This is a common problem—almost every child goes through this phase. This can be even more common in families where corporal punishment is used (physical punishment such as hitting, smacking etc) although it is a fact that this can happen even in families where no corporal punishment is used.

This is my solution to this problem.

- If your toddler is aggressive or resorts to physical violence, avoid labelling the child such as, 'Bad boy/girl' or 'you're naughty' etc.
- Also avoid hitting or smacking the child back. The child will not understand why their parent is allowed to repeat the same action when they've been told off about it,
- Instead of humiliating them, set the tone and the boundary by saying something like, 'I know you are upset, however, I cannot let you hit me/ your friend. I know you are a good boy/girl and you don't want to hurt me/friend. Let's take a few minutes time out to figure out the best way to deal with this'
- Children turn violent because they may be upset about something. Empathise with their upset feelings yet set firm boundaries of what is allowed or not. Do offer to help them find an alternative way to express their feeling.

Case Scenario 31

Why does my child ignore my instructions?

Several parents over the years have asked this question.

One parent especially finds it infuriating when her child ignores her instructions and directions when she is pressed for time.

My way around is the following:

- Try to teach your child to listen to you when you are speaking. If they ignore your normal conversation, they will get in the habit of ignoring your requests.
- Find out if your child has a hearing problem, trouble paying attention or a cognitive condition? If you suspect any of the above, get your child professionally assessed and tested.
- Instead of reacting at the spur of the moment be prepared with steps you can take during situations when you find that your child is acting like they don't hear you when you give them instructions
- Steps to help get your child to listen to you:
    - Remove distractions, such as screens, toys etc.
    - Give one instruction at a time. If you give too many instructions in one go, your child won't remember them, and you will end up repeating yourself again and again.
    - Bring yourself to your child's height while making eye contact with them. This will help them focus their attention on you while you are speaking. If you must give out instructions from faraway, instead of yelling from another room, call or summon your child to you so that you can observe their expressions while you give out your instruction.
    - Ask your child to repeat your instructions

back to you so you know that they have understood them. Not doing this step will give you a 50-50 chance of them carrying out your instructions, as you have little idea whether they have understood what you've just told them. By getting them to repeat what you've told them — it will confirm that they have heard and understood what you've said. This will ensure they are already thinking over how and when to complete their instructed tasks.

- Give them consequences before-hand for failing to carry out your instructions. Caution – There is little benefit when you give unrealistic threats when you have no plans to carry them out. For example, if you want them to put away their clothes that are lying on the floor, avoid threatening them with unrealistic statements such as, 'Pickup up your clothes or I will throw them in the bin!' Will you really throw them in the bin? Instead, saying something like, 'Please pickup your clothes from the floor now or else you will spend the whole afternoon in your room having to tidy up your room.'
- Allow for instances when they won't follow your instructions despite having followed my suggested methods Now what? Remember that children should learn to do things out

of choice. This includes following your instructions. If you've followed my methods correctly and despite that, your child does not complete their assigned tasks that's their choice! However, they also then face the related consequences.

- Always remind yourself and your child that they have a choice—a choice to follow instructions or not—*each choice will have a realistic consequence that your child will face.* Rather than forcing your child to do what you've asked, using the choice method will help teach your child responsibility and accountability.
- Being consistent with this method is crucial as you are teaching your children valuable life lessons in making wise choices and reaping the rewards or making bad choices and reaping the poor consequences.

Case Scenario 32

How might I be inadvertently fuelling my child's misbehaviour

In my experience both with my family and also with my parent clients, well-meaning parents often don't realise that yes they may have children that sometimes misbehave, however they often don't realise that we as parents may largely be fuelling or triggering that misbehaviour. After discussing this subject, a parent was very unhappy to hear this. The Dad could not understand how or why this may be possible? I gave some examples:

- If your child isn't picking up their toys as you previously instructed, you resort to shouting at them, '*WHY* haven't you picked up the toys?! You *NEVER* do what I ask!' Now repeat this statement a couple of times and you are boring into the child's mind that they are inadequate and NEVER meet your expectations therefore they will eventually learn to conclude it doesn't matter whether they listen or not.
- If you tend to have a nervous disposition, for example you get stressed very easily while driving or when your children are around—you will inadvertently give out nervous and stressful vibes to your children and they may tend to become unsure of themselves whenever they are in your company.
- Being over critical of them—Well-meaning parents and carers may think that finding faults with your child in their homework, sports or extracurricular activities etc will help shape them positively and encourage the improvements that you want them to have. However, while constructive criticism is a useful tool to shape and help motivate your child, constant criticism is a danger to them. Frequent fault finding or criticising will result in your child losing their self confidence. This can be detrimental to their

emotional well-being.

- Let them see you fail sometimes—This is just as important as letting them see you succeed. Sufficient and appropriate exposure to your successes and failures teaches them that just like them you are human and make mistakes and get things wrong. However, humility and perseverance teach you to get up, dust off and try again.
- Having high expectations from your children – If your child feels that your expectations are too high for them and they can never hope to achieve them, they will lose heart and not want to persevere. Don't let them give up!
- If you keep changing your instructions or don't follow through with warnings or rewards, you run the risk of inadvertently making the child lose their motivation, joy and self-esteem. They can also become stubborn and hard-headed. Let's face it – these are not qualities we want to encourage!

Case Scenario 33

How can I connect with my child's feelings?

'Form a connection with your child' is a common phrase we hear everywhere in childcare these days.

In my training sessions for parents, we often discuss this topic. When a parent asked me to explain this in layman terms, I explained in the following way, 'A connection is a relationship of mutual understanding between two parties. I gave some examples and tips to this parent on how she could form a connection with her four-year-old child:

- Fill your child's emotional basket every day. Do this by spending one-to-one time with them twice a day, every day. Spend a minimum of 15 minutes with them once in the morning and once in the afternoon. For example, in the morning, set your alarm for 15 minutes earlier and spend some quiet time cuddling your child while they are slowly starting to wake up. Or get ready and leave home a little early for school runs and spend a few minutes in the car talking and listening to them. Spend 15 minutes again in the afternoon after bath time or dinner time, cosy up on the sofa or bed. You could read or play games etc.
- Get into the habit of listening! Attentively listen to your child when they speak. If you have other children as well, make sure to listen to each child at a time without allowing the other to interrupt the conversation. This will encourage your child or children to also listen to you when you speak without distraction and interruption. For example, if one child is speaking to you and another child interrupts you, stop the interrupting child in their tracks, by saying something like, 'Wait darling, let your brother

finish what he is saying first and then you can tell me your story'. Eventually you may find that just holding up your index finger to stop the interruption without saying anything will do the trick just as well. Start doing this as early as possible: the earlier you put this in play, the easier you will find communicating with each child with full attention.

- Observe your child while they play or do any activities. Watching them at play is a remarkable way not just to bond with them but also to learn more about their thought process. When you watch them at play, interact with them, commend them, and gently pull them back on track. Make-believe games and imaginative play are a great way for them to learn things such as problem solving, perseverance and when you observe these things, promptly commend them.

Case Scenario 34

Dealing with an aggressive child

Dealing with an aggressive child isn't an alien concept to me. I am sure it isn't alien to you as well. While we have covered the scenario of a child that hits, we will discuss tips with how to deal with a child that is aggressive most of the time.

A parent recently asked me to give some in depth insights for this.

I gave her the following pointers.

- Aggression can take many forms: Hitting, kicking, scratching pinching, biting, angry outbursts, throwing of objects, shouting tantrums etc.
- This can happen in children who haven't yet learned to understand or control their BIG feelings or their impulses. It could also be that the child may be undergoing some stressful life events such as bereavement, illness, a home-move, or a new baby. It is also possible they may have underlying learning and social difficulties such as autism or ADHD etc.
- One of the first ways you can deal with frequent bouts of aggression from your child is to stay calm yourself. If you lose your cool at every given opportunity, you might be inadvertently fuelling the behaviour. Next, try to determine the underlying cause of this aggression. Are there any life changes as mentioned above? Or is the child going through something more serious in their life and their frequent aggressive behaviour may be a 'cry for help'?
- Help the child to understand and express their BIG feelings in the correct manner. For example, if the child has had a series of late nights and has an aggressive bout triggered by prolonged over tiredness, help the child to settle down first before scolding or disciplining them. If they are hyped up, you scolding them at that moment won't register with them straightaway or help the

situation improve. Instead say something like, 'I understand you are very upset. Let's settle down with a bath and dinner. We can then have a chat about what's upset you'. By doing something like this, you are not just recognising the problem but also removing your child from the situation that has triggered his behaviour. You are also not overlooking or justifying his aggression but plan to deal with it when both your child and you are in a more receptive mood.

Case Scenario 35

Help! What should I know about my teen using social media.

Do you have teenagers and/or preteens? If like me you do, often, you may have been asked this question by them. We are social creatures, and our children are no different. Often, however, our children find them aware of and surrounded by many forms of social media. This can be TikTok, WhatsApp, Instagram, Facebook, Twitter to name a few.

An overwhelming number of parents have approached me in recent years about getting advice on allowing their children on social media.

One of the parents, who didn't consider herself very tech savvy, approached me for advice on dealing with this. She didn't want to come across as, in her own words, 'silly' when talking to her teenagers about social media. But she, equally was interested in how her children were interacting and keeping themselves safe on social media.

I gave her the following pointers.

- Have a family meeting before you decide to allow your child to have their own phone. Make sure you and your spouse are on the same page as, sometimes, one parent can be played against the other. This typically happens surrounding phones and social media.
- Be aware of age restrictions as most social media accounts require the user to be thirteen and above. This is not to say that thirteen-year-olds are automatically mature enough to sensibly use social media platforms. They need education about the benefits and dangers of these platforms.
- Before you allow your child on social media, set some ground rules. Help them to understand that the virtual world can be as dangerous as the physical world. As part of the 'induction period' of social media consider setting a time with your child to attend an online safety awareness course with you.
- If you haven't yet got one, set up a social media account for yourself and follow your child and invite them to follow you too. You and your child will then be 'followers' and an 'audience' on each other's social media platforms.
- Part of the attraction of social media for youngsters is having a large number of 'friends' or 'followers'. While it may seem innocent, help your child to understand that adding any and

everyone to their social media account is unwise. Reason with them, that you wouldn't want to invite any and everyone to your living room at home. The online world is full of unsavoury characters out there under the guise of innocent looking people. They should only add as 'friends' to their social media account people they know in real life.

- Have regular and frequent conversations about their social media 'friends' and conversations etc. Once they appreciate that the topic of social media isn't taboo at home, they will be more likely to approach you with any concerns or questions.

Case Scenario 36

How do I teach my child about online safety

The online world is a world that can be alien to many in our generation.

Many of us can differentiate our online world from our offline world. However our children are growing up in the digital age and they often cannot separate the two worlds.

During my sessions recently, a client parent posed the question on how to keep her two children aged eight and twelve, safe online.

These are following pointers I shared with her..

- Nearly two-thirds of parents don't know what their children are accessing on the internet. Given the choice, most youngsters may prefer interacting with their friends online rather than face-to-face.

- Youngsters are often easy targets for online scammers, hackers, identity thefts, grooming, cyber bullying, pornography, and even online abuse.
- Cyber bullying can be done even through harmless looking apps such as WhatsApp, social media platforms, snapchat I-messages etc. For example, cyber bullying often includes people setting up WhatsApp groups and then adding and removing your child, blocking, and unblocking your child from the groups as 'reward' or 'punishment' for something they've done or said. This can be particularly distressing to your child as they consider their online world to be as important as their offline world.
- Your best port of call would be to have frequent and open communication with your child – even daily. Make no subject a taboo. Discuss things that their friends may be discussing on the day. Ask open ended questions for example, 'What do the kids at school think about pornography?' or 'Have you seen the new challenge of—that is trending online?' etc.
- Once your child starts to open up and reveal something, avoid jumping at or overreacting at what they say. You will want your child to speak freely in a safe environment. This will help you

to understand and help your child tackle the challenges they are facing in the online world.

- Discuss with your child about safe online activities including their phone usage. Set clear ground rules regarding what they can access and not on their screens. Agree with them that you reserve the right to monitor their online activities for their own safety just as you are responsible for them for their offline activities for their safety.
- You may find that you if you try and ban them from using social media or the internet at home or on their phone, they will likely be tempted to access them outside of home where you have little or no control. This can often be even more dangerous as this way they don't want or let you help them navigate their way around in the online world.
- Remember that although your teenagers may know about the online world, you know more about life, hence have the best interests of your child in your heart.

Case Scenario 37

Dangers of Child Exploitation

Child exploitation can be one of the most uncomfortable topics to talk about. In my conversations with parents and carers, often we find that well meaning parents and carers may avoid talking about the subject. However, I believe that being forewarned is forearmed.

Hence, many parents are not sure what they should do if they suspect that their child has been exploited. As exploitation can take many forms and these forms change from time to time, it is important we familiarise ourselves with these forms so that we can quickly determine if our child is at any risk of danger. One parent asked me to list examples of child exploitation:

- Sexual exploitation: Using the child as a victim or pawn of sexual abuse.
- Manipulation: Playing with the child's emotions, blackmailing the child into getting them to do something. For example, 'If you love me, you will not tell our secret'.
- Grooming: Examples can include trying to get close to or curry favour with a child with the intention of winning their trust. For example, repeated gifts, praise and affection can serve as lures to get close to a child.
- Labour exploitation: Forcing them to perform child labour. The child sees no other way out than to slave away to earn money or feed themselves. For example,making the child work in unwholesome conditions just so that they have some money to feed themselves or send money home.
- Child criminality or child soldiers: Blackmailing or brainwashing an innocent child to perform criminal acts. For example, manipulating the child's emotions to perform vengeful acts of harm and violence.

This is in no way an exhaustive list as forms and dangers of exploitations are growing all the time. Our children and teenagers are innocent, naïve, and inexperienced. Therefore, they are even more in danger of exploitation.

Case Scenario 38

Detecting signs of abuse and exploitation

Parents regularly ask me this so that they can be aware of signs and warnings of abuse and exploitation.

A parent recently told me that she knew there were all these dangers around but didn't know how to detect them. She and her husband worked full time. They sent their two children to school and nursery respectively. Some days, their neighbours would pick the children up from school and the children regularly met with extended relatives and family friends on the weekends. The parent understandably didn't want to frighten the children with scary stories of abuse etc, nor did she want to restrict the children's social life and activities. However, she did want some clear-cut guidance to help her and her spouse with this very sensitive subject.

My tips to help her included the following suggestions.

- I commended the parent for taking this topic seriously as this is a difficult and unrated subject. Many parents shy away from being aware of what signs they need to look out for until it is too late.
- Signs you need to look out for are, the child may suddenly become withdrawn, quiet, and

reserved. They may jump or shudder at sudden noises. They may have unexplained bruises or burn marks. This is a fairly common sign of physical abuse.

- Displaying inappropriate behaviour such as dressing or acting in a 'sexualised manner' or involving their private parts.
- Being secretive about their activities such as hiding their phones or messages, spending unusual time on their devices secretly, hiding messages or sneaking up at night or when no one is watching to contact somebody.
- Possessing unexplained gifts or money that cannot be reasonably accounted for.
- Avoiding or unusually seeking out the company of certain people, either online or offline, frequently complaining of feeling unwell to avoid meeting certain people.
- Often children don't know how to express their hurt or feelings of shame. They may write or draw something, which you find unusual or disturbing.
- Nightmares and/or bedwetting, (for younger children)- Older children may display unusual irritability, feeling shame or dirty about themselves.
- Developing eating habits such as becoming unusually fussy with anorexic and/or bulimic tendencies.

While this list is again not exhaustive, it is worth noting that individual signs on their own may not necessarily mean that your child has been exploited, however looking at the individual signs in conjunction with one or more other signs should certainly flag up your concern.

Case Scenario 39

Teaching my child about body consent and personal boundaries

Parents often ask me this question. One parent recently suggested that she feels that she should wait to teach her children about body consent until they're a bit older and can understand better.

The following was my response to her.

- I explained to her that while it is commendable for her to decide to teach this sensitive subject to her children when they are older, I emphasised that it will be in her children's best interests to start at a younger age.
- Even if they are young or learning to speak now, she should start by teach them their proper body parts without skipping any of them. She can do so during bath time or dressing time. It is important that they learn *proper* names rather than so called *childish or street* names for their body parts. This will serve them in good stead as they grow up as this helps them to recognise that all body parts—private or otherwise—have their appropriate use

and function for their bodies to work properly.

- Teach them that their private parts are *private,* not shameful or secret. They can talk about them with Mummy or Daddy or within the family or with the doctor if Mummy and Dad say it's ok. This will help them to recognise that they *can* and *should* raise concerns with their trusted grownups if something is bothering them or something that doesn't feel right.
- From a young age, teach them that they have the right to their personal space or 'bubble'. Nobody should come within their 'bubble' if they feel uncomfortable.
- You should teach them that 'No' means 'No'. For example, they need to respect other's personal space just as well.
- Never ever *force* or *coax* them to kiss or hug someone, no matter how much you or the other person wants them to. Children have good instincts. If they feel comfortable to approach and give someone a hug by themselves, generally it's their instincts telling them that it is ok.
- Teach them the 'step back' method. We teach this method to children as part of body language training to help them regain some control over their surroundings. If they feel uncomfortable or threatened about someone or a situation, children can generally sense it and in that case, we teach them to hold up their hands and step

back. This increases the distance between the child and their perceived danger. This also gives you some insight on the situation and the child's feelings about that situation.

- Teach your child to respect other people's feelings also. If another child or person wants their space or 'bubble' teach your child to allow others their space also.
- Teach your child that it is never ok to keep other people's secrets from you, no matter what it is. Even if the other person threatens, blames or shames the child or makes them feel guilty, tell them that they need to come and tell you. Reassure your child that you will believe them and not blame them.
- Keep your child's trust and your communication open, even daily if possible. If your child feels that they can't trust you even in small things, this will prevent them from trusting you with their big concerns.

Case Scenario 40

Keeping the parenting pressures down during the pandemic

Parenting pressures have greatly increased during the pandemic. While pressures were bad before, they have now become far worse than we could ever expect.

A few families I have worked with have brought their concerns to my attention about how parenting pressures have affected not just their family life, their work, their children but also their own mental health.

During one of the lockdown periods, I had a parent who phoned me in a severely upset state and poured out her heart to me. She just couldn't cope with the pressures of working from home, home-schooling her two children, lack of support and understanding from her in-laws (as she lived in a joint family), demands from her boss as well as trying to cook and manage household chores etc. She was also ashamed to admit that she found herself drinking alcohol every day even during the day to help her 'cope' with her pressures. Also, she had resorted to sleeping tablets at night to help her calm her nerves and sleep peacefully.

All of these problems no doubt took its toll on her.

I listened at length with empathy as in my experience in working with families, this had almost become the 'new normal'.

Of course, there was nothing I could do to physically change her situation. Certainly, I was sure that she was at the end of her tether and could not continue this way for much longer.

I gave some practical tips to help her take the edge of her pressures.

- I advised her to take some alone time for herself twice a day, every day. Even if it was just for 15 minutes each time, it was crucial that she take this time for herself *without* anyone around her. She could go for a walk down the street, sit in her bedroom with the door closed and listen to music or even just go and take a warm shower. Doing this would help clear her head, gather thoughts together and calm her down before things could pile on top of each other.

- If you have several children, agree with any family living with/or near you, to watch the children for you while you take your break. Worst case scenario, put a movie on for your kids, go in the kitchen and make yourself a coffee.
- Do deep breathing exercises twice a day, preferably during your break time. This will help the oxygen to flow into your brain properly, lower your blood pressure and calm you down. Try drinking a glass of cold water every couple of hours as well. Stay properly well hydrated, this will help you keep focussed as well as help prevent the cravings for alcohol.
- Try to break home-schooling into bite-sized sessions—both for you as well as your children. You do not need to sit with them for 6 hours straight to help them study. For older child, try to aim for 45 minutes to an hour at a time; for younger children try 15–20 minutes at time.
- Agree with your spouse and other relatives to take turns to do some chores around the house, whether it is cooking, washing up or laundry etc. Acknowledge your situation – you are not superhuman and you need time and space to yourself to recuperate also.

- Forgive yourself. Sometimes we tend to expect too much of ourselves. In the process, we get disappointed and stressed. These are not normal times, therefore you need to give yourself a break too!

Case Scenario 41

Effective working from home while home-schooling

Whether you have been working from home generally or only during the harsh lockdowns, it is never a piece of cake if you've had to home school your children at the same time. Things can become difficult while trying to manage both tasks effectively.

Last year, during the tensed second lockdown period, I had a zoom meeting with a parent who struggled to effectively manage working from home along with home schooling at the same time. Both she and her husband worked from home during that time and employed a part time house help. They had two children aged five and ten years old respectively.

My suggestions were the following:

- Be structured and organise your day thoroughly. You may be tempted to let things slide and take their own course such as letting the children wake up later or have later mealtimes etc. However, this will be detrimental to your work pattern in the longer run.
- Assign them age-appropriate lessons that should keep them occupied for 30 minutes to an hour

at a time. After that take a 10-minute break with your kids—away from the lessons, have a snack, do your toilet trips etc and then resume their assigned lessons for another 30 minutes to an hour at a time. Do this daily and you will notice that their attention span will increase with each passing day. This will give you time to organise your other work around the school lessons.

- With organisation, consistency is important. Successful and stress free home working and home-schooling won't happen by fluke. You will need to invest a few days helping your kids get organised and adjusted to their home-schooling lessons. Once they are used to the structure and timings, you will find that they adjust more easily to you also working at another task while they complete their lessons.
- While everyone is at home, there is usually that tendency for the family to expect Mum to prepare and provide fancy meals on cue. However, if Mum is also working from home, this is not always possible. Hence, take turns with your spouse to prepare meals. If you have the luxury of a house help, get them to do the food prep while you are working also.
- If possible, keep your work area separate from the living area. The last thing you want is that your employer or clients become annoyed by the constant distractions such as the doorbell ringing

or you having to entertain endless requests from your children. Take turns with your spouse to do lessons with your children at the allocated times while the other attends a work meeting or makes a work related phone call. Similarly, arrange your work meetings and calls away from your children's lessons.

- Avoid all work calls during family times in the evenings. Set aside that time to relax with your family, whether you are watching a movie together or playing games together. Doing this reconfirms to your child that you respect family time and likewise, they will also learn to respect your work times during the day.
- Allow for flexibility—this can be hard if you are like me, wanting your day organised and planned out. However, if you are trying to make a success of home-schooling while WFH, you are bound to come across some hiccups along the way. Instead of getting hung up or stressed by them, use them to do better next time.

Case Scenario 42

Managing multiple children from different age groups during the pandemic

In the same scenario as above, the parent had children of different age groups, whom she found difficult to manage. The parent didn't want to give more attention or preference to one child over the other. The children had a relatively big age gap of five years, which meant that both their needs and demands were remarkably different too.

I empathised with the parent as managing children of different age groups is hard at the best of times. Managing them during a pandemic is even harder with new challenges many of which we may have never faced ourselves.

My advice included the following suggestions.

- To avoid competition between the siblings: Set some one-to-one time aside with each child at least twice a day every day. This time needn't be long, even 15 minutes should do it. It is imperative to allow each child to feel relaxed and comfortable in your company. Try to do an individual activity with them that they enjoy without your attention being divided by another child. For younger children, it could be to play while sitting on the floor with them with cars or Lego. For older children, it could be cooking or baking with them.
- While you are spending time with one child, your spouse can spend one-to-one time with the other child and then swap both children around. This will help both parents to gel with each child individually and will help fill your children's individual emotional basket without feelings of jealousy or competitiveness.
- During sibling squabbles, avoid taking sides with either party. Help to manage conflict kindly

without physically fighting. Only get involved if there is a risk of someone getting hurt.

- Help your children to take turns when speaking, using toys or other items around the house. If you find them snatching, pulling or tugging at something, give them a warning that both will lose the item if they continue snatching. After the warning it is important to then follow through.
- In addition to spending one-to-one time with each child, spend family time together with phones and screens switched off. Playing board games together such as carrom, ludo, card games, monopoly etc. will contribute to teaching them camaraderie, team spirit and people's skills all of which are useful social skills even for grown-ups.
- Allow for disagreements but tell them to handle their disagreements away from the family space. My reason for enforcing this is to help them understand that disputes and disagreements are allowed but that they should do so privately and calmly without creating a scene in front of the whole family or neighbourhood. This will hold them in good stead as they grow older, they will learn to have better control over their emotional outbursts. It will make them capable of handling their emotions in a more sensible manner.

Case Scenario 43

Bringing baby home – first time parents

It can be a daunting task for any parents let alone new parents.

I've recently had some new Mums share their personal struggles, with one parent in particular saying that she felt she couldn't bear to face any new mama groups or spend some one-to-one time with her spouse. She struggled to cope with the sleepless nights, feeding time and in general struggled to bond with her baby.

My suggestions included the following points.

- Try to meet other new Mums at least once a month if you can. Keeping in touch with the outside world and with your older friends will help you start to feel more normal and feel like your own person.
- Labour and birth are a shock not just for you the Mum but also for your new baby. Allow yourself time to recover from the so-called aftershocks to both your bodies.
- Welcome visitors, but try not to let it overwhelm you. It may seem unusual but ask your family or friends to help themselves to cups of tea or cold drinks. No one will mind!
- Avoid inviting visitors during nap times as it will only serve to upset your baby's sleep leading to a much-unsettled baby by the evening. Try not to let every single visitor handle the baby too much. Remember, while in the womb, the baby would be used to sounds but not touch, so try to keep the physical handling limited.

- If you have had a C-section or an otherwise difficult delivery, which has laid you up for weeks on end, do not be afraid to ask for help with household chores, shopping etc.
- Chances are that after your delivery you will likely be on maternity leave and while the initial time off from work may seem like a boon, you will miss having some adult company at home with whom you can converse normally. Have a friend come by during the day to keep you company.
- A new Mum's health (both physical and mental) is usually very fragile straight after birth, hence while your physical health may be cared for, attention to your mental health is just as important. If your baby blues persist or get worse after the first week or so after birth, make sure to speak with your doctor.
- You may have had the best of intentions to breast feed your baby, however if you find that this isn't working out, try and look for support groups where practical help is often provided to help you make a success of breast feeding. Don't settle for old wives tales about breast feeding, do your own research and seek out help if you are struggling. If you decided to bottle feed for whatever reason, try not to be weighed down with guilt. You must decide what is best for you and your baby.
- Try to avoid the trend of harsh diets or strenuous exercise soon after your delivery. Remember

that it took your body nine months of major internal and external changes to go from your normal shape to your post birth shape. Give yourself some time to eat well, exercise without putting new pressures on your body to snap back instantly.

Case Scenario 44

Bringing baby home – Second time and eventual parents

We often assume that if you've had a child before you know all about parenting. This could not be further from the truth. From personal experiences and those of other Mums I've worked with, I know that situations and challenges with your first baby and subsequent babies differ enormously.

One such parent shared their concerns with me during their second pregnancy. She already had a three-year-old toddler, and she was now eight months pregnant with her second child. Her first pregnancy and childbirth were both pretty much straightforward. She didn't have as many sleepless nights as she thought she might have and she also sailed thoroughly smoothly through the feeding and setting of routine etc. Now with baby number two, she found that she didn't have much time to herself having to work as well as take care of her toddler. She didn't have as many rest periods. Her second pregnancy was also not problem-free. She suffered much pregnancy related illness and woes. And she was just dreading what new challenges the birth of her second born baby would bring.

My suggestions to her were the following:

- Try not to worry too much about what will happen after the birth of the second baby. Initially, it may take a bit of effort but eventually, it will get easier having had a baby before. Childbirth and early days will not be a completely alien territory to you. You may find that you may not have to rely entirely on pregnancy books for advice etc.
- When your baby is born, you will naturally want to introduce your toddler to them. After all, you will expect them to excitedly welcome their new sibling and playmate! However, be prepared that this may not always happen. You toddler may not initially warm up to the idea of a 'new kid in town'
- During your pregnancy, get your toddler to feel the baby kick and talk to the baby. I also suggest having some baby dolls for your toddler at that stage so that they can start getting used to seeing their Mummy or Daddy carrying someone smaller than them. Playing dolly games with your toddler, such as helping your toddler to change dolly's nappy or pretend feeding and burping dolly, will help your toddler feel important and involved in the baby's care. After the baby is born, your toddler can help look after their own baby dolly along with Mummy.
- Avoid referring to the new baby as 'Mummy's baby' in front of your toddler. Don't forget your

toddler was your first baby and you don't want them to feel they've been replaced by someone new.

- Your new baby will no doubt be getting many gifts, remember to get plenty of gifts for your toddler as well. Most importantly, at birth, present your toddler with an 'I love you' gift from your new baby. This may sound silly; however, in my experience your toddler sees this as one of the first signs that having a new sibling is positive news for them.
- As soon as you are back home from the hospital, Mums especially should spend some one-to-one time with their toddler *every day* without the baby around. This can be at bath time or bedtime etc. This helps to affirm to the toddler that the new baby has not snatched their Mummy from them.
- Never ever let anyone compare your toddler to your new baby. Comments about facial features or skin tone may seem harmless to well-meaning relatives, however, they can cause lasting damage to both your children no matter how young they are.
- Prop up your toddler's self-esteem by calling them things like 'hero' or 'helping hand' big brother/ sister for their baby and Mummy and Daddy by doing little tasks to help such as bringing a nappy or helping you bottle feed the baby, showing the new baby picture books or toys.

Case Scenario 45

Bringing home baby – New Dads

New Dads often tell me that they feel their role as a new Dad is just a supportive role to their spouse who are left to do the bulk of the adjustment after the baby.

One such Dad aired his thoughts that he wondered what more he could do to contribute other than the occasional nappy changing or bottle-feeding duties.

My suggestions were the following:

- New dads should encourage the new Mum to meet other fellow Mums when she feels up to it. Try to help her become mobile so she doesn't feel stagnated at home day-in-and-day-out. Avoid coming home late from work. Remember, your spouse would have spent the whole day with the baby. She would love nothing more than some adult company in the evenings.
- In addition to being involved with changing and feeding. If your spouse has mastered the breast-feedings aspect, try not to feel left out, you can be involved in other things such as burping, changing or preparing formula if you both decide to bottle feed. Try to help with night feeds with expressed milk even if mum is feeding the baby during the day.
- As before, stay involved in the process from the beginning. Helping bathing or dressing the baby can be a big relief to a new Mum. Keeping things ready for the bath and/or change of clothes is useful also.

- Try to help with the shopping, cooking, clearing up, laundry. You might also find that your partner may appreciate a few minutes every day to herself to have a shower or even a cup of coffee in peace. Be proactive, not reactive.
- As much as you may want to show off your new baby, just be mindful that it will be physically very draining for the new Mum as well as the new baby to be entertaining visitors for long periods of time. This will be especially true if the new Mum has had stitches and bruises. It can make sitting or standing for long periods very difficult. Be considerate of these conditions. Whenever possible, ask your visitors to arrange a time before hand when both baby and Mum have rested enough.

Case Scenario 46

Raising an 'able' child – Finding out if your child has special needs

In some parts of the world, an 'able child' can generally be described as someone who has special talents or abilities or somebody with a 'can do' attitude. This is often contrary to the view held by many that an 'able child' is someone who has certain skills and abilities that overshadow his or her social or communication abilities. For example, a child may have outstanding creative and imaginative skills, but they may shy away from the usual social interaction in groups or mainstream education. Or a child may have unusual mathematical or musical talent but may under perform in other fields such as literacy or language.

Often, individuals who tick boxes tend to be on a genius level or have an ability in which they outshine most of their peers. However, we as human society put great emphasis on fitting our child into a certain mould that society considers more appropriate. And when they don't conform to those standards set by society, we often worry that something may not be right or normal with our child.

One such situation came to my attention, wherein a set of parents had a very talented daughter who was four years old at the time. She excelled in her creative and imaginative skills. However, she just could not concentrate on her education as she grew up. She could never learn her multiplication tables or remember spellings. She also developed some problematic behavioural traits which her teachers and parents found very frustrating to deal with. After observing her, I suggested to the parents to get her professionally evaluated to rule out certain learning difficulties such as are frequent in Autism, Asperger's and ADHD. Thankfully, they took my advice and found out that she did indeed show signs of mild non-verbal Autism.

Understandably, they found this news challenging to accept and blamed themselves for the girl's condition. They felt that their child's handicap was a result of their parents having done something or not having done other things to help the situation.

The following ideas were my tips to them.

- Give yourself time to accept that it is natural and ok to feel upset if your child has been diagnosed with a learning and/or social difficulty. I would consider it wrong to suggest that parents should pretend that nothing has changed. If we do find a situation challenging, it will help us become more resilient to life's changes and 'rise' to that challenge.
- Allow yourself to go through a whole range of emotions such as shock, disbelief, anger, frustration, blaming each other etc. These are normal feelings, part of th e process of coming to terms with the condition. Here it is key to remember that you and your spouse come out the other side feeling more positive and confident with a new plan in your parenting journey.
- Understand that your child is 'unique' and has their own individual personality traits, talents and failings. They should never feel that they are being compared to their peers.
- Avoid expecting them to behave exactly as how you perceive other children their age behave or respond. No two children are ever the same, especially when they have differences in personalities, learning, socialising etc.
- While it may be a shock for you and your spouse, chances are that your child may have already noticed that they are somewhat different from

their classmates or peers in some ways. They may even blame themselves for their perceived differences. However, remember that they now need you to be their rock and support even more in every way.

- Never allow negative comments from well-meaning family and friends to bring you down. Having a child is a blessing, having a special child is a special blessing.

Case Scenario 47

Raising an 'able' child – Accepting and adapting

Following from the previous case scenario, finding out if your child has special needs is one thing, accepting and adapting your parenting method to the new situation is another. When parents ask me for suggestions on adapting, I give the following pointers.

- Understand that an 'able child' doesn't automatically grow out of their special needs. Nevertheless, they can learn ways to harness their learning difficulties as they grow older and go out into the world.
- Help them socialise with people who *they* feel comfortable with. It is no good forcing them to mix with a certain age group of peers as this may make them feel out of place and in turn lose their confidence in themselves.
- Depending on their level, they will understand better when you speak to them in short and direct

sentences. They often have difficulty focussing on many things, people, even words. Keep your instructions short and repetitive.

- Maintain eye contact with them. Children in this spectrum cannot cope with too many instructions or many visual changes all at once. In order to get their attention, get to their level, look at them, call their name to hold their attention. Speak to them in short sentences.
- If your child is at the high end of the spectrum of their special needs and you worry about taking them on outings with family or in crowds, consider getting them used to noise cancelling headphones. This will help them to focus on one thing at a time – whether it is listening to their favourite songs or a favourite audio story, headphones are useful to keep them happy and content for short periods of time.
- All children thrive in a good, consistent routine, children with special needs even more so. Have fixed timings for their meals and activities, use labels, pictures and other visual aids if needed to help them anticipate their next activity.
- On the other hand, if you find that there is a break in their routine, they may find it particularly difficult to cope, so much so that they may even feel as if their whole world has collapsed. Try to avoid any break in their routine.
- Contrary to popular belief, children with special

needs can be very affectionate and loving. The only difference is that they may have different ways of showing it. Don't hold back your affection from them. Be alert to never say anything in front of them or to them which may make them feel unloved or unwanted.

- Children with special needs may also go through frequent spells of anxiety. Depending on the severity, they may display anxiety in unusual ways such as through their hands and mouths. Chewing on your hair may be sign of seeking out comfort, repeatedly tapping their knee or hitting their head may be a sign of frustration etc.
- To help them cope with this, get them into the habit of carrying their favourite doll, cuddly toy or blanket as a comforter or soother. No matter how old they get, they will benefit from having a form of comforter that they can instantly use to soothe themselves.

Case Scenario 48

Raising an 'able child' – Along with their sibling(s)

Okay, now that you have got a framework of how to adapt yourself to a child with special needs, what if you are a parent who has other children. How do you successfully manage both parenting styles for each child?

One such predicament was brought to me by a parent who really struggled to maintain the right balance with her older child who seemingly didn't require as much attention as her younger child who was diagnosed with ADHD.

In fact, the parents were doing remarkably well with helping their younger special child adjust and adapt to society and mainstream education. Yet, they were struggling with behaviour problems of their older child who didn't seem to have any of the special educational needs that his younger brother had. They felt that the older son wasn't being supportive enough, he was rebelling more often, answering back, having fits of anger, showing outright disobedience, flunking at school etc.

My observations included the following points:

- The older son seemed to be playing out his frustration at his parents through his behaviour. His 'rebellious behaviour' was a cry for some attention from his parents.
- He understood that his younger sibling had special needs that required to be dealt with differently. Yet he also felt that his parents would often take out their own frustrations with the younger child on him due to no fault of his. It was worse when they expected him to understand and accept it.
- There were also times when the tired and guilt-ridden parents would buy extravagant gifts for their older son as a way of compensation for not giving him enough attention.
- He often felt more of a 'babysitter' than a 'sibling' of his brother. His parents also expected *him* to always make compromises with things in favour

of his brother.

- All of these things no doubt caused a form of resentment and friction to build up between the brothers but also between the older son and his parents.
- He found that the only way he could get them to pay attention to him was through bad behaviour. And the attention he got was not the good kind. This no doubt became a vicious circle which started to spiral out of control.

My tips were the following:

- I advised the parents to, without delay, set aside some one-to-one time with the older son twice a day, every day. They could take turns each time, with either mother caring for the second child and the father spending time with the older son and vice versa. Spend this time doing something positive together with the older son such as, playing football in the park, going out for a walk, video games, anything. without any interruption from the younger child. Even if your older son protests against this persevere, it *will* produce results.
- Take opportunities to praise the older son to your younger son, such as, 'Wow, look how well he laid the table!' or, 'He brought your comforter to you; he is such a kind big brother isn't he?' Regularly and genuinely praising children in front of each

other helps build their own self confidence and also helps build appreciation between children.

- Listen calmly and respectfully to your child's feelings and opinions. It helps them feel valued and gives them a sense of belonging. In this case scenario, part of the problem was that the parents were too tired dealing with the special needs of their younger child and they had no energy to spare to be patient and understanding with their older son. It was not fair to expect him to step up and show maturity every time when he himself was only a child who also needed the time and attention from his parents.
- Accept help or better still, ask for it. Ask family and friends to pitch in and help out with childcare taking turns with the children. This will ensure that you are able to spend time with both children giving them your undivided attention while retaining your own energy resources.